Robinson Public Library District
606 North Jefferson Street
Robinson, IL 62454-2699

The IRS And You

The IRS And You

How To Play The Game And Win

Joseph F. Zerga, M.S., CPA
and
Richard J. Bannon, Ph.D., CPA

Mainstream Press
584 Castro Street, Suite 518
San Francisco, CA 94114 USA

Copyright © 1996
by
Joseph F. Zerga and Richard J. Bannon

All rights reserved. No part of this book may be reproduced or transmitted in any form or by any means, electronic or mechanical, including photocopying, recording or by any informational storage or retrieval system without permission in writing from the publisher.

Published by Mainstream Press, 584 Castro Street, Suite 518, San Francisco, California 94114 USA.

Cover design by Don Mooring

ISBN 1-881943-04-6

Library of Congress Catalog Card Number: 95-80429

Printed in the United States of America

"—Oh dear, how puzzling it all is! I'll try if I know all the things I used to know. Let me see: four times five is twelve, and four times six is thirteen, and four times seven is—oh dear!"

—Lewis Carroll, Alice's Adventures in Wonderland

Contents

Introduction		9
Chapter 1	The Tax Audit Lottery	11
Chapter 2	Correspondence, Office and Field Audit	19
Chapter 3	Who Should Represent You in an Audit	25
Chapter 4	Administrative Appeals and the Tax Court System	37
Chapter 5	Collections	47
Chapter 6	Interest and Penalties	55
Chapter 7	Statute of Limitations	67
Chapter 8	Problem Resolution Program	73
Chapter 9	Offer in Compromise	77
Chapter 10	Trust Fund Recovery Penalty	83
Chapter 11	Bankruptcy	89
Chapter 12	Fraud	111
Chapter 13	Resources	119
About the Authors		123
Index		125

Introduction

This book is about you, the American taxpayer and the Internal Revenue Service. Its purpose is to unravel the mystery of an IRS audit and explain your rights as a taxpayer. It can be fairly said that the IRS has an advantage since it not only makes and administers the rules but is also a full time player of the game. However, by understanding the administration of the federal income tax system, you should dramatically increase your level of confidence and sophistication in dealing with the IRS, and thereby create a more level playing field.

Equally important to understanding the audit process is a comprehension of related matters such as interest and penalties, dealing with the IRS when you owe tax but do not have the money to pay it, tax liens and levies, tax fraud, etc. These areas and others have also been addressed.

Hopefully, this book accomplishes the dual purpose of explaining the rules, procedures, and practices of the IRS in a straightforward manner and providing you with insight on how to improve your position each step of the way. Of course, these rules, practices and procedures may change over time. Thus it would be advisable to consult with a knowledgeable accountant or attorney to determine their current status before relying on their application to your particular situation.

CHAPTER 1

THE TAX AUDIT LOTTERY

How Your Tax Return Is Selected For Audit

How To Avoid Having Your Tax Return Audited

The Tax Audit Lottery

After you file your federal income tax return with the Internal Revenue Service (IRS), what are the chances that you will be selected for audit? Fortunately, the IRS has limited personnel and resources available, so only a small percentage of all returns filed can be selected each year for actual audit by an IRS agent. Therefore, the IRS is pressed to make its selection very carefully so as not to waste time auditing returns that will not bring in additional taxes. How does it go about doing this?

First Stop—Internal Revenue Service Center

When you file your tax return, you send it to the Internal Revenue Service Center designated for the place where you live. The Service Center has the first opportunity to check out your return. It does this by putting it under the scrutiny of both a manual examination and a computer processing program. All returns go through this process.

Check Point #1
(Errors, Unallowable Items, Bad Matches)

Initially your tax return is assigned to a tax examiner at the Service Center for a manual review. As part of this review, the tax examiner converts the information on the return to numbered codes which are entered on a magnetic tape which is then run through a computer processing program. What kind of errors are being searched for in both the manual and computer inspection procedures?

The IRS has developed a number of general programs aimed at identifying various kinds of tax return errors which will result in the assessment of additional tax. Among these programs, there are three which appear to be the most significant and widely used:

1. the Mathematical/Clerical Error Abatement Program
2. the Unallowable Items Program

3. the Information Returns Program

More specifically, these programs are geared to detecting the following types of errors which may appear on your return:

Mathematical Errors: Errors in addition, subtraction, multiplication, or division; also, errors in computation of percentage limitations on deductibility of certain items such as medical expenses, casualty losses and certain miscellaneous itemized deductions.

Clerical Errors: Omission of information required to substantiate a return item (for example, the documentation required to verify the value of property contributed to charity); use of the wrong IRS table in computing the tax (for example, where the return for a single individual uses the tax rate table for a married person filing a joint return).

Unallowable Deductions: Deduction of items which, by their description on the tax return, are not allowable deductions (such as deductions for political contributions, or charge card interest expense incurred on the purchase of personal items, etc.)

Discrepancy between Return Items and Information Returns: The amount reported on the tax return as dividends, wages, proceeds from stock sales, mortgage interest, etc. is matched to W-2 forms supplied by employers, and 1099 forms supplied by banks and other third parties. Any discrepancies will be detected.

If this examination process comes up with mathematical errors which clearly understate the tax on your return, you can look for a tax bill to show up in your mail.

If the problem arises due to apparent clerical errors, a discrepancy which shows up in matching your return items with information returns, or a deduction on your return which appears to be unallowable, the Service Center will usually make a further decision as to whether your return indicates a strong likelihood for substantial tax changes. If so, your return will be sent to your IRS District Office to handle the examination. Otherwise, the Service Center will send you a letter with the proposed adjustment in your tax and with a request that you either agree to the adjustment or explain why you believe the adjustment is wrong. If you agree and pay the tax, in most cases (but not all) that will be the end of any examination of your tax return and you can breathe a sigh of relief. If you disagree and your letter of explanation fails to provide satisfactory reasons for your disagreement, then you can expect further action by the IRS.

Your tax return may have run this first stage of IRS review successfully without any additional proposed tax assessment; however, your return has not necessarily escaped further attack from the IRS. There are two other special programs to which your tax return might fall prey.

Check Point #2
(The Discriminant Function System—DFS)

Under the DFS program, the tax return is run through a computer program which applies a mathematical formula to the various line amounts on the return. Based on knowledge acquired through experience, the IRS has developed a secret mathematical formula which assigns various numerical weights to the absolute and relative amounts of various items (such as gross income, interest expense, charitable deductions, amount of refund claimed, etc.) and to the types of items (such as nonbusiness bad debts, tip income, or worthless stock losses) on tax returns. As explained earlier, when the initial tax examiner at the Service Center manually processes your return, he/she pencils in numbered codes for the various items on your return.

The penciled codes are entered on magnetic tape and scores are computed and compared with a predetermined minimum level.

If your return scores below this minimum level, you have escaped the shadow of audit under this program. If it scores above this minimum level, it joins all the other returns with high scores which are then subjected to another manual inspection to take into consideration other aspects of the return which cannot be measured by the mathematical program. For example, a large charitable deduction for a property contribution may cause or contribute to a high score; but the manual inspection may show that this deduction is clearly supported by reliable appraisal reports included with the tax return. The IRS recognizes that it does not have enough revenue agents to audit all of the tax returns whose scores exceed the minimum level. Thus the objective of this manual inspection is to select those which have the clearest potential for the highest additional tax revenue.

If this process results in a judgement that your return shows promise of a substantial additional tax assessment, it is sent to the appropriate district office to be considered for audit.

Jack and Jill Fail the Test

Jack and Jill report gross income on their tax return of $25,000. They also report $15,000 in charitable contributions and $10,000 in interest expense paid on their house. Since it is not logical that they would spend 100% of their income on mortgage interest and charities (leaving no money for food, clothing, medical expense, etc.), their tax return would not pass the DFS program.

Check Point #3
(The Taxpayer Compliance Measurement Program)

With the Taxpayer Compliance Measurement Program, you just have to depend on the luck of the draw (i.e., not to be drawn).

The Taxpayer Compliance Measurement Program takes an entirely different approach. Periodically (historically between periods of two to four years) the IRS audits a random sample of individual income tax returns. For example, in November 1994 the IRS announced that it would apply this audit program to 1994 returns and would randomly select 153,508 returns nationwide to examine line by line. The objective of the program is to measure how well (or how poorly) taxpayers are doing in reporting their proper income and deduction items, in paying their taxes in a timely fashion, and in supplying any required supplementary information. This is a complete audit and the IRS agent must scrutinize every item on the tax return. The results of this audit are used to update the DFS program. If your return happens to fall into the net of this program, that's the luck of the draw. Be prepared to support every line item on your tax return.

Check Point #????

There are, of course, a number of other reasons why your return could be selected for examination. For example, the IRS may arbitrarily decide to audit a certain percentage of tax returns with gross income of $250,000 or more. Also, when a refund claim is filed, the Service will generally take a closer look at the return for the year involved, and this increases the likelihood of audit. Another roadblock—the IRS frequently selects specific businesses and occupations for more intensive audits, particularly where cash transactions are heavily involved (e.g., used auto dealers, restaurants, liquor stores, attorneys, etc.).

Next Stop—The IRS District Office

If you fail to get by any of the above checkpoints at the Service Center, your return will be sent to your IRS District Office. However, this still does not necessarily mean you will be audited.

Each year the National Office of the IRS coordinates the planning for deciding the number of returns which should be audited. This is based largely on the number of IRS agents available. However, the number of returns sent by the Service

Centers to the District Offices for potential audits is not limited to this budgeted number. Indeed, the District Offices generally receive far more returns than they can possibly audit. Therefore, the District Office will weed out certain returns to reduce the actual audits to a manageable level.

Of course there are some returns, such as those selected under the Taxpayer Compliance Measurement Program, which they may be required to audit. The other returns are reviewed manually and are ultimately selected for audit based on their potential for tax increases. At this stage, particular items on the return to be considered in the examination may be earmarked, and the type of audit (correspondence, office, or field) will be established.

The District Office, for a number of other reasons, may also request the returns of specific taxpayers from the National Office. For example, informants may report suspected fraud. Another reason for examination of a particular taxpayer is the link that the taxpayer has to other returns, as when an IRS audit of a corporate return may disclose that the corporation paid a substantial amount of personal expenses of its president. This may lead to an examination of the president's personal tax return to determine whether those amounts were included as taxable income.

To Summarize

There is no way to absolutely ensure that your tax return will not be selected for audit. You can, however, greatly reduce your chances by taking the following steps:

1. Make sure the mathematics are correct. Double check your addition, subtraction, etc. Also make sure you use the correct tables in computing your tax.

2. Provide all the supporting information the IRS requires. Make

sure you attach your W-2 form to the return.

3. Explain, in detail, any large or unusual items on your tax return. If you take a deduction for a theft loss, explain exactly what happened.

Good News/Bad News

The good news is that probably only 1% to 1.5% of all tax returns filed each year get audited. The bad news is that over your lifetime there is approximately a 50% chance of getting audited. However, since the IRS does not waste time auditing tax returns that show a small amount of income, the higher your income, the greater your chances of being audited.

CHAPTER 2

CORRESPONDENCE, OFFICE AND FIELD AUDIT

The Difference Between The Three Types Of IRS Audits

How To Handle Each Type Of Audit

Correspondence, Office And Field Audit

The Burden Is On You
(Unlike a Court of Law)

Unlike a court of law, where you are presumed innocent until proven guilty, the burden of proof is on you in an IRS audit. An IRS audit, simply stated, is a civil administrative procedure where you, the taxpayer, justify the items that you have reported on your tax return. If you cannot provide the information to justify these items, the IRS will disallow the deductions and assess additional tax. Internal Revenue Code Section 7602 (Examination of Books and Witnesses) clearly establishes the right of the IRS, in assessing the correctness of a tax return, to:

1. **Examine books, papers, records, etc.**

2. **Summon the person liable for tax, or any other person the IRS may believe has relevant knowledge etc., and take the testimony of any such person.**

After your tax return has been selected for audit, the IRS will notify you in writing. The letter you receive from the IRS will further advise you of the type of audit you are to be subjected to—specifically, correspondence, office or field audit.

At this point, you will feel that you have been culled from the herd of taxpayers and targeted. Keep a handle on yourself; the overwhelming majority of audits are routine administrative examinations. You are not being audited for fraud and you are not going to jail. The IRS expects a large percentage of returns, selected for routine examination, to be adjusted either for an increase or decrease in tax. Remember, your return was probably selected because the IRS perceived an opportunity to increase tax revenues, not put you in jail.

Correspondence Audit
(The Easiest)

A correspondence audit is usually the simplest form of audit. The letter you receive from the IRS will either:

a. Request additional information from you or,

b. Propose a change to your return.

If only a few items are being questioned on your return and the items questioned appear to be fairly simple to answer, a correspondence audit is the fastest way to resolve the problem. Essentially, this is a verification of record keeping, and the IRS will request that you mail certain information that verifies an item(s) on your tax return. For example, the IRS may request a copy of the year-end statement you receive from your mortgage company listing your mortgage interest expense.

Very often people forget to include certain items in their tax return. It is very easy to overlook small amounts of income such as interest from a savings account. Since the IRS matches correspondence from the bank (miscellaneous income is reported on Form 1099 by the bank to the IRS) with income reported on your tax return, the omission will be detected. You will receive a letter from the IRS **proposing** the addition of income and income tax. The proposal is in the form of a bill. If you agree with the change, simply sign the form where indicated and write a check to the IRS for the amount billed, and the correspondence examination is over.

But beware: what starts out as an ordinary correspondence audit may blossom into an office or field audit. The IRS will refer your case for either an office or field audit if it is not satisfied by correspondence. Similarly, you, the taxpayer, may request that your return be referred for either office or field examination if you do not agree to a proposed correspondence change to your tax return. It is definitely in your best interest to keep what starts as a correspondence audit from becoming either an office or field audit. Office and field audits are more comprehensive.

Office Examination
(Worse)

For more complex tax returns requiring an advanced knowledge of tax law and the exercise of judgement, an office audit is scheduled. The IRS will send you a letter that has been generated by a computer. The letter will tell you to call the IRS office to schedule an audit date (the IRS prefers to use the word "examination"). If the time scheduled for your audit subsequently turns out not to be convenient, you have the right to request that the examination be re-scheduled. Generally, the IRS is very reasonable about re-scheduling.

The letter you receive will ask you to provide specific records and documents that support and verify items that are being questioned on your tax return. For example, the IRS may ask you to verify all medical deductions you have taken on your return. You would support these deductions by producing canceled checks, paid receipts, etc. The total amount of the receipts and canceled checks should be equal to the amount reported on the tax return. If you cannot support a deduction you have taken with a canceled check or other receipt, the IRS agent will disallow the deduction and increase your tax liability.

Office audits are scheduled by IRS agents throughout the day. Further, the agents are under a certain amount of pressure to complete the audits that they are assigned as quickly and efficiently as possible. It is in the best interests of you, the taxpayer, to assemble neatly all of the data requested so that you can complete your audit in one interview. If the IRS agent feels it is necessary to schedule a second interview, the audit may expand to other items on your tax return.

Field Audit
(Worst)

Field audits are scheduled when the tax return is complicated and requires IRS agents with a knowledge of accounting matters as well as tax expertise. Field audits ordinarily (but not always) focus on corporation and business returns.

Unlike an office audit where only certain items are selected for examination, the IRS agent in a field audit will usually take a comprehensive approach and examine the entire tax return in detail.

A field audit, as the name implies, is conducted on the premises of the taxpayer. Unlike office audits that require establishing appointments throughout the day, the field auditor has fewer time constraints. If necessary, the IRS field auditor can spend days (or weeks) in your office (or home).

Because the IRS agent has the luxury of time, and because field agents are the most sophisticated auditors, these audits are potentially the most dangerous. If possible, try to shift the field audit to the offices of your tax representative. This strategy has the advantage of having a tax professional answer IRS questions (as opposed to employees unskilled in tax matters). If it is not possible to change the location of the audit, request that the IRS agent deal exclusively with your tax representative during the audit. All document requests should be made in writing by the IRS agent. Only your tax representative should be responsible for complying with these requests. Advise employees not to deal directly with the IRS agent, but to refer all questions to your tax representative. The greatest source, by far, of additional audit revenues is produced by field audits.

Industry-Specific Expertise
(Market Segmentation Specialization Program)

In order to effectively audit various industries, the IRS has recently developed industry-specific audit guides. These guides are the result of comprehensive research by the IRS and are used to give auditors expertise in a particular industry. Without a doubt, these audit guides give the IRS a powerful and dangerous new audit tool.

Guides currently exist, or are being written, for such diverse businesses as attorneys, architects, insurance agencies, jewelry dealers, mortuaries, plastic surgeons, and used auto dealers.

Remember

Advance preparation and knowledge is of paramount importance for surviving an IRS audit. Forewarned is forearmed.

CHAPTER 3

WHO SHOULD REPRESENT YOU IN AN AUDIT

Who Should Not Represent You In An Audit

The Foolish Attorney Represents Himself

How To Manage Your Tax Audit

Your Rights In An Audit

Who Should Represent You In An Audit

(Not You, the Taxpayer)

Generally, the three types of professionals who can (and should) represent you in an IRS audit are attorneys, certified public accounts, and enrolled agents. These individuals have completed substantial educational and licensing requirements.

Circular 230

Circular 230, published by the Treasury Department, establishes the rules that define and govern those professionals who can practice before the IRS. The purpose of Circular 230 is to protect both the taxpayer and the IRS by requiring that persons who represent themselves as tax practitioners have met certain minimum standards of technical competence. In accordance with Section 10.3 of Circular 230, Attorneys, Certified Public Accountants, and Enrolled Agents may practice before the IRS. The rights bestowed on these individuals include:

> "...the preparation and filing of necessary documents, correspondence with and communications to the Internal Revenue Service, and the representation of a client at conferences, hearings and meetings."

Other commercial tax preparers may accompany tax preparers to audits, but do not have the broad authority granted to Attorneys, CPAs, and Enrolled Agents.

Attorneys

Not all attorneys are tax attorneys. In fact, the majority of attorneys have minimal knowledge of tax law. In certain areas of taxation, where in-depth knowledge is required, an attorney who specializes in a particular area of taxation should be consulted, otherwise a certified public accountant or enrolled agent is probably your best bet. Attorneys who do practice tax law generally have a masters degree in taxation or a specialized tax background such as IRS work experience.

Certified Public Accountants

Certified Public Accountants (CPAs) are licensed in all states, territories and the District of Columbia. CPAs are required to have a college degree, work experience, and are required to pass a stringent national examination administered by the American Institute of Certified Public Accountants. Additionally, most states require that CPAs complete a certain number of continuing education hours each year.

While the CPA exam contains a section on taxation, and most people tend to associate CPAs with the preparation of their tax returns, in fact many CPAs do not do tax work. Their time is spent preparing or auditing the financial statements of companies and providing other types of accounting and advisory services. Those CPAs that do tax work are usually very good, and have a broad knowledge of accounting as well as tax. For the majority of audits, particularly audits that involve accounting issues, a CPA would be the professional of choice.

Enrolled Agents (EA)

Enrolled Agents are tax practitioners who have either completed a comprehensive examination in taxation administered by the IRS or have been employed by the IRS for a minimum of 5 years. Enrolled agents are not required to have a knowledge of accounting.

PERSONALITY TYPES TO AVOID
(The 4 C's)

Cowboys

This personality type is over-aggressive, argumentative and confrontational. They like to treat IRS agents as if they were spotted lepers. If possible, during an audit, they will seat the agent on a rickety card table next to the bathroom door. Ultimately, this strategy will back-fire and create an unnecessary antagonistic atmosphere. The agent may decide to get over-aggressive and you, the taxpayer, will be the target.

Cowards

This type is intimidated by the IRS, afraid to take a positive position with regard to an item on your return that is being questioned by the agent. They are quick to point out that they have not audited or reviewed the information on your return, but simply prepared the return based on information you have provided. Advocating your position is simply not their cup of tea. At heart they are bookkeepers and will agree with the IRS whenever possible to avoid controversy.

Conduits

Conduits are messengers. They want your business but they don't want to do the work. During your audit the IRS agent may send lists of items they want substantiating income and deductions that you have reported on your tax return. The conduit will hand this information over to the IRS, without review. In many ways the conduit is the most dangerous of the personality types to avoid. They are non-professionals posing as professionals. Any professional worth his salt will scrutinize every scrap of information before giving it to the agent.

Classicists

Classicists are like classical music pieces; they never change. They have not kept up with the changes in the tax law and are technically obsolete.

THE FOOLISH ATTORNEY REPRESENTS HIMSELF

After you receive a letter from the IRS advising you that your tax return has been selected for audit, you can either represent yourself during the audit or hire a tax expert to represent you. The best argument for representing yourself is that, at least in the short run, it may be cheaper. Beware, however, that this may be a penny-wise and pound-foolish decision.

More Damage Than Good

There is a lot of truth to the old saying that "a lawyer who represents himself has a fool for a client." The potential to do yourself damage by meeting an IRS agent is, by far, greater than any potential you might have to improve your position. Rarely, if ever, should you represent yourself in an IRS audit or even speak on the phone with an IRS agent.

You Are Not a Tax Expert and May Be Emotional

Not only do you not have the technical tax knowledge to deal effectively with a professional IRS agent, you may inadvertently say something that hurts your position. You would be amazed at how many people have gotten themselves into serious trouble by thinking they could "just sit down and explain everything to the IRS agent." Further, people are far more emotional about their own money and this can only complicate the audit.

Into the Lion's Den

Very often taxpayers become fascinated with their audits and insist on accompanying their tax representative to the audit. The wise tax representative will immediately discourage the idea. He knows that the IRS agent will direct all questions to you, the taxpayer. The IRS knows that you will be nervous and unskilled in tax matters. The IRS also perceives that a personal confrontation usually means an instant answer to almost any question and therefore is the quickest way to complete the audit. Inevitably, the IRS agent will assume control of the audit, and the tax representative will become a spectator.

The shrewd tax representative also knows that a certain fact pattern may be expressed in different ways. Therefore, it may be advisable to think a day or two (or do additional tax research) before answering a particular question posed by the IRS agent. This potential time lapse, and it is a big advantage, is lost when you, the taxpayer, insist on going to the meeting with the IRS.

MANAGE YOUR TAX REPRESENTATIVE IMMEDIATELY

In these days of independent professionals and voice mail, communications with any professional are, at best, often frustrating. It is therefore to your enormous advantage to come to an understanding with your tax representative as quickly as possible in order to avoid the "they won't even return my phone call" syndrome.

The Squeaky Wheel Gets Greased

Almost all professionals develop a sixth sense about prospective clients. This sixth sense is an invaluable tool to a professional. It tells the professional:

Who Should Represent You In An Audit

- Whether or not you will be a difficult client to deal with in terms of emotions, cooperation and reasonableness.

- How sophisticated you are about taxes and your audit.

- How likely you are to pay your bill on a timely basis.

It is important for you to present a cool businesslike image to your prospective tax advisor.

Before you select a tax representative, do:

- Consult friends and business acquaintances about tax advisors of whom they have knowledge.

- Find out what your prospective tax advisor's educational and work background is.

- Find out who will actually conduct your audit. In larger firms the work may be done by a subordinate after the initial interview. If a subordinate will do the work, ask to meet him.

- Ask for a quick, off the cuff, review of the items the IRS is asking you to produce. This will give you an idea of how difficult the audit will be.

- Find out what hourly rates are charged by the firm. Also ask for an estimate of the total cost. Naturally, this can only be an estimate. The total cost, depending on how the audit goes, could be higher.

- Tell your prospective advisor that you will assemble and organize all the data that the IRS requests. This includes proof of mortgage interest paid, donations, interest income, etc.

- Tell your advisor that you will keep phone calls to a minimum, but that you do not expect to play phone tag.

- Make it clear that you want a **detailed** billing that includes not only time spent, but what the time was spent on.

After you have selected a representative, do not:

- Pay a substantial "retainer fee" to begin the case.

- Make a pest of yourself and spend unnecessary time on the phone.

- Bring a shoebox full of information for your advisor to sort through. They hate this type of work and may charge punitive fees to do it.

- Cancel appointments unless absolutely necessary.

- Be lazy about assembling the information your advisor requests.

YOU HAVE (SOME) RIGHTS
(A Small Step in the Right Direction)

In 1988, Congress approved a so-called "Taxpayer's Bill of Rights." These "rights" are enumerated in IRS Publication 1 (also available in Spanish) entitled "Your Rights as a Taxpayer." Authored by Senator David Pryor of Arkansas, the "Bill of Rights" is intended to reduce abuse of taxpayers by the IRS. In recent years the IRS has made an effort to become more user-friendly with the American public. In this spirit, the very first sentence of Publication 1 states:

"As a taxpayer, you have the right to be treated fairly, professionally, promptly, and courteously by Internal Revenue Service employees."

What Rights Do You Have?

The "Taxpayer Bill of Rights" does, in fact, provide both psychological and strategic benefits. The most important include:

Privacy and Confidentiality
(Sometimes)

You have a right to privacy with regard to your tax return. It is not a matter of public record. Beware however that, within the framework of legal guidelines, the IRS can (and will) share your tax information with State tax agencies and other Federal agencies such as the Department of Justice. However, the person who prepared your tax return must treat it as a confidential document. You also have the right to know why the IRS is asking for certain information from you, what they plan to do with the information, and what happens if you refuse to give them the information.

Courtesy and Consideration
(Psychologically Gratifying)

Agents must treat you in a courteous and considerate fashion. No more psychological dominance. If you feel you have not been treated in a fair and courteous fashion, you have the right to speak with the agent's supervisor.

Repeat Examinations
(Relief from being Double Dipped)

If you are one of those unfortunate souls who seem to get audited every year, there may be some relief. You may request (and usually the IRS will comply) that any item on your return that has been examined during the two previous years, and no change has been proposed, be deleted from the audit. If the only items being proposed for audit are those that have previously been audited—without change—then the entire audit may be canceled.

Protection of Your Rights
(Somewhat Vague)

Employees of the IRS are supposed to "explain" and "protect" your rights at all times. This concept is a little unclear—however, there it is.

Complaints
(You can Complain)

If you have a complaint about how you were treated you may write to the District Director or Service Center for your area or the IRS will supply you with a toll free number. Bear in mind, this is not to be used as a means to express your dissatisfaction with the outcome of an audit.

Representation
(This is a good one)

You can have a lawyer, CPA, or Enrolled Agent represent you in your absence. You must sign Form 2848—"Power of Attorney" authorizing a tax advisor to represent you in your absence. This is an important strategic tool!

Recording
(Not Recommended)

You can make an audio tape recording of the interview (or request your tax representative to do so) by providing your own equipment and giving the IRS 10 days written notice. Likewise the IRS may record the interview by giving you 10 days written notice. If the IRS requests a taped interview, consult an attorney or CPA immediately. Demanding that the interview be taped will likely irritate the agent and certainly guarantee a formal rather than relaxed atmosphere. Besides, there is no assurance that you will like what gets recorded.

Stop the Audit
(I want to get off)

If you represent yourself (not a good idea) and during the examination you feel yourself getting into deep water, you can stop the audit, seek professional tax help and re-schedule. However, the IRS will not stop the interview if you are there because of an administrative summons.

Explanation of Changes

If the IRS proposes to change your tax return, they must do so in writing and explain the reasons for the proposed changes.

The IRS Has Rights Too

If you decide to represent yourself, try very hard to keep your interview with the IRS agent on a professional level. Do not become emotional and argumentative. Remember, it is the job of the IRS to collect exactly the tax that you owe, and not a cent more. Also remember that in a self-reporting system the burden is on you to justify each and every line item on your tax return. If you cannot do this, the IRS has the right to adjust your tax return.

CHAPTER 4

ADMINISTRATIVE APPEALS AND THE TAX COURT SYSTEM

The Thirty Day Letter

Administrative Appeals

The Ninety Day Letter

The Court System

Administrative Appeals And The Tax Court System

The Thirty Day Letter

If at the end of your IRS audit you do not agree with the proposed adjustments made by the IRS agent to your tax return, you will receive a "thirty-day letter." This letter is formal notification of the findings of the IRS agent and asks you to agree with the findings of the audit. If you do not agree with the proposed adjustments to your tax return, you have thirty days from the date of the letter to request a conference with an appeals officer.

Appeals
(Santa Claus is Coming—Maybe)

Not infrequently, taxpayers do not agree with the IRS agent who audits their tax return. To reduce the expense of both money and time spent on litigation, the IRS has established an appeals division. It is the job of the appeals officer (who is also an IRS agent) to act in a strictly impartial manner to both the government and the taxpayer in order to settle tax disputes. The appeals division is the only means of appealing an audit within the IRS. If you cannot solve your problem here, the next stop is the court system.

The setting is informal and the appeals officer has "exclusive and final authority" to settle cases and may use substantial "personal judgement." The reason for the disagreement must fall within the framework of the tax law. You cannot appeal your case because of religious, moral, political or other similar reasons. No settlement will be offered based on nuisance value or when a taxpayer's position is clearly contrary to tax law. An appeals officer is not required to settle a case.

Jack and Jill and the Dog
(A Sad Story)

Jack and Jill loved their dog Spot. Spot traveled everywhere with them and only ate the best food. Spot, in fact, was treated more like a child than a dog. When Jack prepared their tax return, he listed Spot as a dependent; when Jack and Jill's tax return was audited, the agent disallowed a deduction for Spot. Jack protested and took his case to the Appeals Division. The Appeals Officer also dismissed Jack. There is no provision in the tax law for listing a dog as a dependent. Jack had to pay the additional tax assessed by the IRS agent plus interest and penalties.

Jack and Jill and the Cleaning Business
(A Glad Story)

Jack and Jill decided to start a carpet cleaning business. Business was brisk and it seemed they were constantly out of carpet shampoo and other supplies they needed to clean carpets. Jack was always in a hurry and not a good bookkeeper. He threw away all the receipts for the cleaning supplies. When Jack and Jill were audited, the IRS agent disallowed the expense deductions for carpet cleaning supplies because they could not be supported by canceled checks or paid receipts. Jack knew that a tax deduction for supplies was legal and took his case to the Appeals Division. The Appeals Officer was sympathetic and understood that supplies were a necessary expense of the carpet cleaning business. The Appeals Officer and Jack were able to agree on a reasonable expense deduction for supplies on Jack's return. The Appeals Officer advised Jack to keep better records and not to throw away receipts in the future.

If the proposed change in tax (either increase or decrease) is $2,500 or less, you may orally request a conference with an Appeals Officer. If the change is more that $2,500 but not more than $10,000, a brief written statement outlining the issues is required. If the proposed change is more than $10,000, the IRS requires you to submit a statement containing the following information:

1. Your name and address

2. A statement that you want to appeal the examination findings to the Appeals Office

3. The date and symbols from the letter showing the proposed changes and findings you disagree with

4. The tax periods or years involved

5. An itemized schedule of the changes with which you disagree

6. A statement of facts supporting your position on any issue with which you disagree

7. A statement stating the law or other authority on which you rely

You must declare that the statement of facts under (6) above is true under penalties of perjury.

Ninety Day Letter

If you cannot reach an agreement after a conference with an Appeals Officer, you will receive a "Statutory Notice of Deficiency", more commonly known as a ninety day letter. You have ninety days (150 days if you live outside the United States) to file a petition for a redetermination of the deficiency with the Tax Court. If you do not file suit in the Tax Court within ninety days, you cannot contest the deficiency without first paying the tax and then filing a suit for refund in either District Court or the Court of Claims. Ordinarily, the IRS will not make any collection effort during the ninety day period. It is worth noting that the IRS simply has to mail the ninety day letter to your last known address. Moving and leaving no forwarding address will not do any good.

The Tax Court
(Specialist in Tax Matters)

The Tax Court of the United States specializes in tax cases. The judges are appointed for a fifteen year term by the President of the United States. Judges are chosen based on their experience and knowledge of tax law. As previously discussed, for the Tax Court to hear a case, a petition must be filed within the ninety day letter time frame.

Advantages of the Tax Court

1. You do not pay your proposed tax prior to entering this court system.

2. Tax court judges are sophisticated in tax matters so if you want to argue a technical tax issue, this is probably the best forum.

Disadvantages of the Tax Court

1. Interest and penalties continue to add up while you argue your case.

2. If you have an "emotional case", you are not likely to find very much sympathy in this court.

Usually, after the case has been scheduled for hearing in the Tax Court, or other court, a final attempt at a pre-trial settlement will be attempted with an IRS attorney and an Appeals Officer.

District Court

The U.S. District Courts are another court system that hears tax cases. The district court judges, however, are not tax specialists like the tax court judges. District court judges hear all sorts of cases including bank robberies, etc. To have your case heard in District Court, you must first pay the disputed tax liability and then sue the government for a refund.

Advantages of District Court

1. Unlike Tax Courts, you may request a jury trial. This could be a useful strategy if you have an "emotional case" as opposed to a "technical tax case."

2. After you pay the disputed tax liability, penalties and interest stop accruing.

Disadvantages of District Court

1. You have to pay the disputed tax before you can enter the court system.

2. If you have a good technical case, you may want to be in Tax Court.

U.S. Claims Court

U.S. Claims Court hears cases concerning monetary claims against the federal government. The U.S. Claims Court, unlike the District Court System, does not allow jury trials. Like the District Court, however, you must first pay the disputed tax and then sue for a refund. Claims Court judges, like District Court judges, are generalists and not tax law specialists.

If you lose your case at either the Tax Court, District Court or Claims Court level, and believe the lower court erred in its decision, you may appeal (with cause) the lower court decision to the U.S. Court of Appeals having the appropriate jurisdiction.

The U.S. Courts of Appeal

The U.S. Court of Appeals is a federal appellate court. There are thirteen Courts of Appeal. Eleven of the courts are geographically located and assigned a number, one court is assigned to Washington, D.C. and one is for the Federal Circuit. For example, the first circuit includes the states of Maine, Massachusetts, New Hampshire, Rhode Island and Puerto Rico. California, Hawaii, Nevada and several other states are in the ninth circuit. Each circuit court is independent of other circuit courts. This is important because a similar fact pattern regarding a tax issue may have been decided differently in different circuits. For example, the first circuit court of appeals may have decided in favor of the taxpayer regarding a particular type of tax deduction, and the ninth circuit may have decided in favor of the IRS for a similar deduction. Thus, there may be judicial inconsistency among taxpayers.

Decisions of a district court are generally appealable to the Court of Appeals for the circuit in which the district court is located. Appeals from the Tax Court, on the other hand, are generally made to the Court of Appeals for the circuit in which the taxpayer's legal residence is located. U.S. Claims Court decisions can be appealed only to the Court of Appeals for the Federal Circuit.

The only higher court in the United States is the United States Supreme Court. Because the Supreme Court only has time to hear a few tax cases each year, the court of appeals is usually the last authority in the matter.

The United States Supreme Court

The United States Supreme Court is both a Court of Appeals and the highest court in the country. The Supreme Court consists of nine judges and hears cases only in Washington, D.C. The right to have a case heard by the Supreme Court is not guaranteed. Because of obvious time constraints, the Supreme Court can only hear a few cases each year. Therefore, the cases to be heard are carefully selected.

Best Advice

Try and settle your tax dispute with the IRS without going to court.

Do Not Ignore The IRS

Sometimes it is tempting to ignore correspondence from the IRS. This is a big mistake. The IRS has the right to move you through the system if you do not cooperate or respond to their requests. You can be sure that in the process the IRS will maximize their position, and not yours.

Jack and Jill Ignore the IRS

Jack and Jill received a letter from the IRS stating that they were being audited. The letter requested that they schedule an appointment and bring evidence supporting certain deductions they had taken on their tax return. Jack and Jill ignored this letter and several subsequent letters requesting an appointment. Finally, the IRS agent simply disallowed the deductions and assessed additional tax. They received a "Thirty Day Letter" and ignored it. They then received a "Ninety Day Letter." The "Ninety Day Letter" also was tossed in the trash. Jack was shocked when the IRS filed a lien on his house and levied his bank account. Jack's CPA explained to Jack that his only recourse at this point was to pay the tax plus penalties and interest and then file a claim for refund in either District Court or Claims Court. Filing a petition in Tax Court was no longer an option since the "Ninety Day Letter" had been ignored.

The System Diagramed

Diagrammatically the process for final determination of a tax issue is as follows:

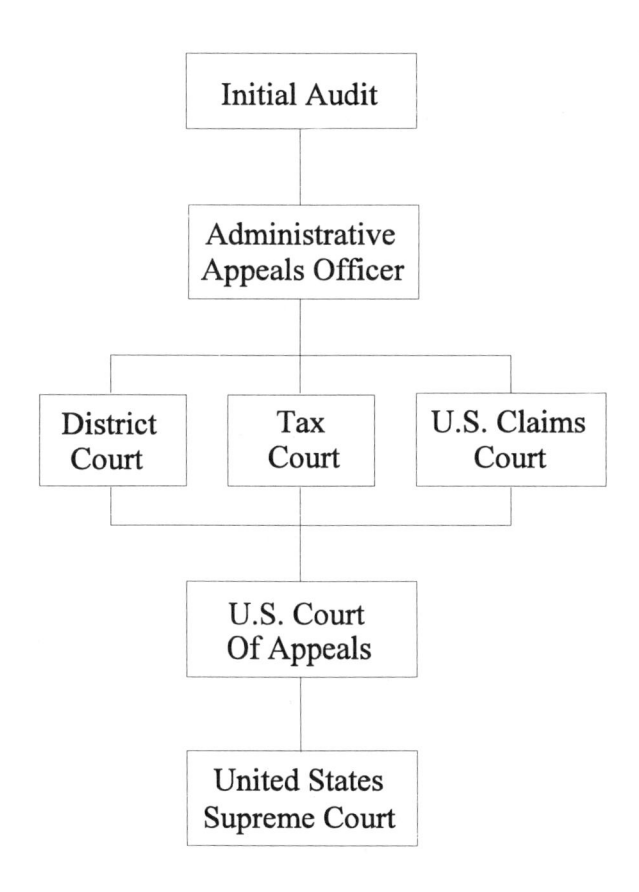

```
                    ┌─────────────────┐
                    │  Initial Audit  │
                    └────────┬────────┘
                             │
                ┌────────────┴────────────┐
                │   Administrative        │
                │   Appeals Officer       │
                └────────────┬────────────┘
                             │
         ┌───────────────────┼───────────────────┐
    ┌────┴─────┐      ┌──────┴──────┐     ┌──────┴──────┐
    │ District │      │    Tax      │     │ U.S. Claims │
    │  Court   │      │   Court     │     │    Court    │
    └────┬─────┘      └──────┬──────┘     └──────┬──────┘
         └───────────────────┼───────────────────┘
                             │
                    ┌────────┴────────┐
                    │   U.S. Court    │
                    │   Of Appeals    │
                    └────────┬────────┘
                             │
                    ┌────────┴────────┐
                    │  United States  │
                    │  Supreme Court  │
                    └─────────────────┘
```

CHAPTER 5

COLLECTIONS

Installment Plans

Liens

Levies

How To Release Liens And Levies

Collections

(What Happens if You Cannot Pay Your Taxes)

Do you go to jail?

Commonly, people do not pay their taxes because they spent the money on something else. Does this mean you can go to jail for not paying your taxes? Except for fraud, the answer is no. The United States does not incarcerate people for non-payment of debts. With few exceptions, (i.e. non-payment of child support) debtors prisons are a relic of the past. If you cannot pay your taxes in total when they are due, it is possible to work out a payment plan with the IRS. Otherwise, they will seize your property and sell it.

Installment Plans

The IRS is generally willing to enter into an installment agreement in order to liquidate a tax liability. They will ask you to complete form 433A (or Form 433B for a business). Forms 433A and 433B are financial summaries. They list all your assets, liabilities, income and expenses. After the form is completed, the IRS, and not you the taxpayer, will evaluate your financial status and decide how much you can afford to pay each month.

The IRS will want their money as rapidly as possible, usually within one year. They will ask you to sell or re-mortgage your home, sell other assets, borrow money or use any other legal device available to raise money and extinguish the debt. They may even ask you to re-arrange your life style. For example, they may ask you to move into a cheaper apartment or house in order to increase their monthly installment.

Even if the IRS does enter into an installment agreement, the agreement may not be final. The agreement will only stay in effect if you:

1. Gave the IRS correct information about your finances when you entered into the agreement.

2. You do not miss an installment.

3. You pay other tax liabilities on a timely basis.

4. You provide more current financial information if the IRS requests it.

5. The IRS decides that the ultimate collection is not at risk.

Make no mistake, the IRS is not in the banking business and they do not like to extend credit. As a practical matter most installment agreements that fall apart do so because taxpayers get lax about making payments on time.

You Can't Get Blood from a Stone

If you have no assets and either no job or a low paying job, the IRS will temporarily delay collection until your financial position improves, then pounce. Naturally, penalties and interest will continue to mount up.

Enforced Collection Action

If you have ignored your tax bill and the IRS believes it can collect money from you, the following steps will be taken in sequence.

Step 1: File a Notice of Federal Tax Lien.
Step 2: Send a Notice of Levy
Step 3: Seize and sell your property.

Liens
(Security for the Tax Obligation)

If the IRS assesses additional tax and dutifully sends you a notice and demand for payment and you ignore or otherwise fail to resolve the tax problem, the IRS will file a lien for the amount of your tax liability. A lien is a claim used to secure a tax debt and establish priority status among other debtors. It serves as formal notice that the IRS has a security interest in your assets. The lien attaches to all of your assets including your house, car, and other real and personal property. A notice of federal tax lien is not valid until it is filed in the county or state where you conduct business. A federal tax lien will definitely have an adverse impact on your credit rating.

Once a lien has been filed, it will be removed within 30 days after you either pay the tax due or post a bond that will guarantee payment. Additionally, the IRS will add to your tax bill the costs charged by the enforced collection action.

Levy
(Seizure of the Property)

A lien is a formal claim to secure a tax debt; a levy is a legal device to actually take the property.

The IRS may levy any property including your house, car, boat, cash value in insurance policies, money owed to you or even your wages. If you live in a state that has state income taxes, they will levy any tax refund check due you.

Certain minor assets such as personal effects up to $1,650, unemployment benefits, certain pension benefits, workman compensation, and wages that have been already earmarked for child support by the court are excluded from levy.

Steps the IRS Must Take

In order to take levy action the IRS must:

1. Assess the tax and send you a "Notice and Demand" for payment.

2. You must ignore the demand or otherwise refuse to pay the tax.

3. The IRS must send you a final Notice of Intent to Levy **at least thirty days** in advance of the actual seizure of your property. However, if the IRS perceives that their economic position is threatened, they can immediately seize the property. The thirty day window is an important time period that should be used wisely. Do not wait until the last minute to try and solve the problem.

If the IRS levies your bank account, the bank is required to hold the funds for twenty-one days. Again, this extended time period allows you to resolve your tax problems with the IRS. After twenty-one days, if the problem is not resolved, the IRS gets the money.

How to Get the Levy Released
(Difficult but not Impossible)

1. You pay the tax plus interest and penalties.

2. You provide the IRS with a plan that will improve their position. For example, you have a large inventory of merchandise that could be sold for a profit. The resulting cash could then be used to pay the tax bill. The IRS will likely remove the lien so the property can be sold.

3. The levy is creating an economic hardship (see section on Problem Resolutions).

4. You enter into an installment agreement with the IRS to make payments. Beware, however, the IRS will not do the same deal twice. Once you enter into an installment agreement you must stick to it.

5. The value of the property exceeds the amount of the levy and the release of part of the property would not hinder the collection of the tax.

Seized and Sold

After your property is seized, the IRS will give public notice, usually in a newspaper in the area, where the sale is to be held. After notice (except in the case of perishable merchandise) you have ten days before the sale to redeem your property by paying the tax or making other arrangements to settle the liability. If real estate is sold, you have six months after the sale to release the property by paying the purchaser the price paid for the property plus interest at 20% annually.

Bottom line—What are the choices?

If you cannot pay your taxes, you have the following choices:

1. **Enter into an installment agreement.** The IRS must be convinced that you will have sufficient surplus cash to pay off the debt in the near future.

2. **Try to work out an offer in compromise.**

3. **Lay back and let the IRS seize and sell your property.**

4. **File for protection under the federal bankruptcy laws.**

While this move will definitely stop all IRS action, it requires consultation with an attorney who is familiar with bankruptcy law. The subject of bankruptcy is discussed in detail in Chapter 11.

CHAPTER 6

INTEREST AND PENALTIES

How Much Interest And How Is It Calculated

Penalties In Addition To Interest

How To Avoid Both Interest And Penalties

Interest And Penalties

(Interest on the Tax, Penalties on the Tax, Interest on the Penalties—When Does it All End?)

The IRS places a premium on filing tax returns accurately and paying tax on time. If you fail to do either of these properly, you will be subject to both interest and penalties. The IRS says, in effect, that if you did not pay your tax on a timely basis, then you were borrowing money from the U.S. Government.

Naturally, if you overpay your tax, you will be entitled to a refund; and you may or may not be entitled to interest on it. However, the IRS will pay you less interest than the interest it charged you when you owed tax.

INTEREST

When? Under what specific circumstances will you be charged interest?

How Much? How does the IRS determine just how much interest?

Refund? If you have a refund coming because you overpaid your tax, how does the IRS determine whether you will receive interest and, if so, at what rate?

When Does the Interest Charge Apply?

Estimated Tax Penalty: Technically this so-called penalty is not referred to as interest; nevertheless, its method of computation makes it the equivalent of interest. So for our purposes, we will cover it here.

Our Federal income tax system is on the pay-as-you-go method. Thus most of your income tax for a given year is generally required to be paid regularly during the year as you receive the income. For salaries and wages, this is accomplished largely

Interest And Penalties 57

through your employer's withholding of tax out of your wages. However, many sources of income may not be subject to any withholding or insufficient withholding to satisfy the tax liability in full (e.g., dividends, interest, self employment income, etc.). To cover these situations, taxpayers are generally required to pay "estimated tax" at specified dates during the year, sufficient to bring their total withholding and estimated tax payments to an amount equal to a given percentage (currently 90%) of the ultimate total tax liability for that year. If you fail to meet these requirements on time and do not fall within any of the special exceptions (which are beyond the scope of this book) you pay a penalty which is computed like an interest charge. This can get complicated, so see your accountant.

Regular Interest Charge: The regular interest charge picks up where the estimated tax penalty leaves off. It applies whenever you fail to pay any portion of your total income tax by the date it was due. There may have been good reason for your failure to pay, such as you were in the intensive care unit at the hospital; however, any reason for the failure to pay is irrelevant so far as the interest charge is concerned. The imposition of the interest is **mandatory** under the tax law.

Thus you will be charged no interest unless you have failed to pay the full amount of your income tax liability by the due date of your return (for calendar year taxpayers, by April 15th of the following year). Interest is charged on any underpayment for the period starting only from that date until actual payment.

In this regard, take special note of one point that is often misunderstood. It is a simple matter for you to get an automatic extension of time for filing your return. For example, assume you get an automatic extension of time from April 15, 1995 (initial due date) to August 15, 1995 for filing your calendar year 1994 return. This **does not** give you any extension of time for payment of the tax, but rather only extends the time for filing the return! Any tax due must be paid when the extension is filed. If there is any unpaid tax balance after you file your automatic extension, interest will be charged on the unpaid balance from April 15, 1995 (the original due date for the return) to the date it is paid.

How Much—What's the Rate?

For many years the interest rate charged on underpayments was a predetermined fixed rate, so you could know in advance what the rate would be. Now, however, the rate is adjusted every calendar quarter to equal the "Federal short-term rate" plus three percentage points (rounded to the nearest full percentage point). For this purpose, the "Federal short-term rate" is based on the average market yield on outstanding marketable obligations of the United States with remaining periods to maturity of three years or less. Application of this statutory formula has resulted in various interest rates during the past few years from 7% to 9%. Further, interest is compounded daily. So the effective rate is somewhat greater than the stated interest rate.

Refunds—How About Interest on Your Refunds? (How much do you get?)

If you have made an overpayment of tax and you claim a refund for the overpayment when you file your return, you may be entitled to receive interest on the amount of the refund. However, the Government has given itself a break here. If you file your return on or before the original due date for your return (usually April 15th) and the refund is paid to you within 45 days after the original due date, you get no interest on the refund. If you file your return after the original due date, the Government has 45 days after the date the return was filed to pay you your refund without interest.

An additional Government plum! The rate of interest paid on your refund is one percentage point less than the rate the

Government charges on underpayments of tax for the same period. The statutory formula is the "Federal short-term rate" plus two (versus three) percentage points.

Another point worthy of note! Interest you receive on your refunds is taxable income; but interest you pay due to late payment of your tax liability is generally **nondeductible**.

PENALTIES
(Usury in Disguise)

It is very difficult to argue with the concept that interest should be paid on money that is owed. After all, interest is nothing more than rent paid for the use of someone else's money. The U.S. Congress realizes that tax increases are politically unpopular and that there is a limit to the rate of interest charged for the nontimely payment of taxes before the cry of usury is heard throughout the land. The clever solution is to create another form of punishment called penalties. Penalties are not additional taxes nor are they interest. They are, well, penalties, and they come in many forms.

Essentially these penalties relate to:

- Late, or no, filing of returns

- Late payment of tax, and

- Understating the tax liability on returns filed.

The specific penalties, however, can be complicated and their detailed analysis is beyond the scope of this book. Nevertheless, the book would not be complete without a brief discussion of them.

Failure to File Your Return by Due Date, Including Extensions

For calendar year taxpayers, which includes most of us, our annual federal income tax return for a given calendar year is due by April 15th of the following year. If you're not prepared to file your return by that date, you can easily get an automatic extension to August 15th or even later, if you have a good reason for the delay. But let's assume you don't file by April 15th and you don't get an authorized extension of time to file; you do, however, ultimately file your tax return late and pay any remaining tax liability. You will, of course, be charged interest on the late tax payment. In addition, the IRS may assess you a penalty of 5% per month, up to a maximum of 25%, of the amount of tax liability not paid by the original due date of the return. You may be able to avoid this penalty, however, if you can show that your late filing was due to reasonable cause rather than willful neglect.

Failure to Pay Tax Shown on Return Timely

You do file your return by the due date, including any extension; but you have not paid your tax in full by the prescribed April 15th payment date. Once again, unless your failure to pay your tax on time was due to reasonable cause, and not due to willful neglect, the IRS may assess a penalty. The penalty in this case is 1/2% for each month or fraction thereof (up to a maximum of 25%) that such failure to pay continues.

It is quite possible that the failure-to-file penalty and the failure-to-pay penalty may both apply for a given taxable year. For example, the failure to file penalty of 5% per month can apply to the first five months (i.e., up to a maximum of 25%). The penalty to pay of 1/2% per month can also apply to the first five months, as well as an additional forty-five months (i.e., up to a maximum of 25%). In this case, the amount of the failure to file penalty (the 5% penalty) for a given month is reduced by

Interest And Penalties   61

the amount of the failure-to-pay penalty (the 1/2% penalty) applicable to such month or months. The following experience of Jack and Jill illustrates the interplay of these two penalties, along with relevant interest charges.

Jack and Jill
File Late and Pay Late

Jack and Jill's 1993 Federal income tax return was due on April 15, 1994. However, by filing the appropriate application (Form 4868—Application for Automatic Extension of Time to File U.S. Individual Income Tax Return), they obtained an extension to August 15, 1994 to file their return. This didn't, of course, give them any extension of time to pay their tax but merely an extension to file their return.

Jack and Jill went on a month's vacation at the end of July 1994 and forgot all about filing their 1993 return. Early in 1995 it dawned on them that they still hadn't filed. So they struggled to get their information together and finally filed the return on March 12, 1995. The return showed a balance of tax due in the amount of $10,000.

They sent a check for $10,000 along with their return, in payment of the balance of tax due. On June 12, 1995 the IRS sent them a Notice. In effect the notice said:

1. You owe **interest** on the amount of the $10,000 net tax due, which you paid when you filed the return on March 12, 1995. This tax was due on April 15, 1994, the original due date of the return. So the interest will run for the period from April 16, 1994 to March 12, 1995, the date you finally paid it.

2. Your return was due, under the extension, by August 15, 1994. You didn't file it until March 12, 1995. So unless you

can show reasonable cause for your failure to file on time, you also owe a **late-filing penalty** of 5% a month (maximum of 25%) on the amount of the $10,000 tax due with the return. Since you filed your return six and a fraction (rounded to seven) months after the extended due date, your penalty is limited to the maximum of 25% of the $10,000.

Additionally, the amount of this penalty is also subject to an **interest** charge for the period from August 15, 1994 (your extended due date of return) to June 12, 1995 (the date of our IRS Notice and Demand to you).

3. We realize that you are being charged interest in item (1) above on your late tax payment of $10,000. Nevertheless, unless you can show reasonable cause and not willful neglect for your failure to pay your tax on time, you also owe a **failure-to-pay penalty** of ½ of 1% per month (maximum 25%) of the $10,000 tax due paid late with the return. Your failure ran from April 15, 1994, when the tax was due, to March 12, 1995, when it was paid. This was a period of ten months plus a fraction; this is rounded up to eleven months. However, since you are also liable under item (2) above for the 5% penalty for failure to file for five months included within this same period, your failure-to-pay penalty for those five months will be used to reduce your penalty for failure to file for those same months.

There will be **no interest charge** on this penalty, as long as the penalty is paid within ten days of your IRS Notice and Demand.

What do all these charges add up to? **$3,592.** Here's how the IRS would arrive at that amount. It will take a little extra concentration to follow this (see next page).

Interest And Penalties

Interest on Tax Deficiency:

$10,000 @ 7% (assumed rate)
compounded daily from April 16, 1994
to March 12, 1995 (331 days) . . . . $ 657

Failure to Pay Penalty:

Amount of tax deficiency $10,000
Penalty rate (11 mos x ½%) 5.5%
  Amount of penalty 550

Failure to File Penalty:

Amount of tax deficiency $10,000
Penalty rate (5 mos x 5%) 25%
  Amount before reduction 2,500
Less reduction by amount of
  failure to file penalty for
  five months:
    $10,000 x (5 x ½%)   250

Amount of penalty 2,250

Interest on Failure to File Penalty:

$2,250 (failure to file penalty)
  @ 7% (assumed rate) compounded
  daily for period from August 15,
  1994 (extended due date of return)
  to June 12, 1995 (date of IRS
  Notice and Demand)—301 days   135

TOTAL AMOUNT OWED . . . . $ 3,592

Failure to Pay Tax Required, But not Shown, on Return

Suppose you have filed your return and paid your tax liability in full, as shown on your return. Subsequently, the IRS audits the return and determines that you owe an additional $3,000 of tax. It sends you notice of your tax deficiency and demand for your payment of it. If you pay the tax deficiency within ten days of the date of the notice and demand, no penalty is applied under this provision. If you fail to pay within ten days, the IRS may assess a penalty of 1/2% for each month (or fraction thereof), up to a maximum of 25%, for which the failure continues.

Again the penalty can be avoided if you can demonstrate that your failure to pay the tax within the ten day period was due to reasonable cause, and not due to willful neglect.

Jack and Jill
Their Return is Audited

Jack and Jill filed their 1994 return and paid the tax shown on the return on time. In 1996 the IRS audited the 1994 return and assessed them an additional $1,000 of tax (plus interest from April 15, 1994). The assessment came in the form of an IRS Notice and Demand for Payment, dated September 1, 1996.

If they pay the assessment by September 11, 1996, there is no additional penalty under this provision. If they don't pay until, for example, July 28, 1997, the IRS may assess the 1/2% penalty for the period from September 1, 1996 to July 28, 1997, a period of 10 months plus a fraction. So if assessed, the penalty would be 1/2% per month for 11 months, i.e. $55 ($1,000 x 5½%).

The Accuracy—Related Penalty

In addition to the foregoing penalties, you may be subject to a 20% penalty on the portion of any underpayment of your Federal income tax which is attributable to any one or more of the following causes:

1. **Negligence or disregard of rules and regulations.** This covers such actions as careless or slipshod tax return preparation, failure to keep adequate records to substantiate return items, and careless or intentional disregard of tax rules.

2. **A substantial understatement of the tax.** For individual taxpayers, the understatement is substantial if it exceeds the greater of (a) 10% of the tax required to be shown on the return; or (b) $5,000. In applying this test, however, the amount of understatement is reduced by any portion attributable to items for which there is either: substantial legal authority for the taxpayer's treatment; or the relevant facts are adequately disclosed in the return and there is a reasonable basis for taxpayer's treatment of the item.

3. **A substantial valuation misstatement.** This occurs when the value of any property claimed as a deduction on your return is 200% or more of the amount determined to be the correct amount of value or amount basis. For example, if you claim a deduction of $100,000 as market value for a painting you found in your attic as a charitable contribution of property, and the fair market value is ultimately determined to be $50,000 or less, this will be a substantial valuation misstatement. However, the 20% accuracy-related penalty will not apply under this provision unless the underpayment of tax due to all substantial valuation misstatements for the year exceeds $5,000.

Obviously, all three reasons could apply to the same portion of any underpayment of tax in a given situation. For example, a given underpayment could result from **negligence** in **substantially overvaluing** the amount of a casualty loss, resulting in a **substantial understatement** of tax in the amount of $20,000. Although all three reasons apply to this underpayment, there would be only one 20% penalty applied: 20% of $20,000 = $4,000).

Frivolous Returns

Occasionally some taxpayers find humor in filing a tax return which purports to be a return for Federal income tax purposes, but which is determined to be due to a frivolous position or a desire to impede administration of the Federal income tax laws. In this case, an additional penalty of $500 may be assessed.

Fraud

If it is determined that the failure to file a return is due to fraud, the failure-to-file penalty is increased from 5% to 15% for each month or fraction thereof, up to a maximum penalty of 75% (rather than 25%). This is a civil penalty, which may be imposed in addition to any criminal penalties which may apply.

Similarly, if any amount of an underpayment of tax with respect to a filed return is due to fraud, a penalty equal to 75% of such amount will be added to the tax.

The subject of fraud is discussed in detail in Chapter 12.

Can I Bargain?

While the imposition of interest is statutory and cannot be waived by the IRS, penalties can be waived. Very often the IRS is willing to waive penalties as a bargaining tool in order to resolve an audit with a taxpayer.

CHAPTER 7

STATUTE OF LIMITATIONS

Three Year Statute Of Limitations

Six Year Statute Of Limitations

No Time Limit In Some Cases

Statute Of Limitations

(How Long Does This Go On?)

At Least Three Years

Once you've filed your Federal income tax return, how long will it be before you can be reasonably confident that you won't be hit with additional tax for that year? The **general** rule is that the IRS has the period of three years **after** your return is filed to assess additional tax.

If you file your return on or before the date it is due, this three year period begins on the day after the due date. For example, if you (like most individuals) are a calendar-year taxpayer, your return is due by April 15th for the previous year. If your return for 1994 is filed on any day between and including January 1, 1995 and April 15, 1995, the three year period begins April 16, 1995. Thus the IRS generally would be required to assess any additional tax for that year by April 15, 1998.

If, however your return for 1994 is filed after April 15, 1995 (whether or not you have been given an extension for filing), the three-year period begins on the day after it is filed. For example, if your return is filed May 13, 1995, the IRS would have until May 13, 1998 to assess additional tax for 1994.

In the event you may wish to challenge an IRS assessment for a given year as being outside the three-year period and, therefore, invalid, you will need to be prepared to establish your date of filing. For this purpose, your tax return is considered received by the IRS on the date it is postmarked by the post office, rather than on the date the IRS actually receives it.

Could Be Six Years

The three-year period is the general rule which will apply in most cases. However, there are some circumstances in which the IRS has a longer period of time to audit your tax return and assess a deficiency. It could happen that you innocently overlooked some income you received or believe that certain amounts you received are not taxable income. For example, you receive a large settlement in a lawsuit for lost wages due to your being fired unfairly by your former employer. Believing that this settlement was nontaxable, you failed to include it as income on your return. In this case, the statute of limitations will be extended to six years if the amount of the income omitted is greater than 25% of the actual amount of gross income reported on your tax return.

For example, assume your actual income for the year is $100,000, including $22,000 from the above lawsuit settlement. The gross income reported on your tax return amounted to only $78,000 ($100,000 minus $22,000). The amount left off, $22,000, would be 28.2% ($22,000/$78,000) of the amount of income on the return. Since 28.2% exceeds 25%, the statute of limitations would be extended to six years from the date the tax return was filed.

There is a way to omit income from your return which you believe to be non-taxable **without** exposing your return to the possible application of the six-year limitation period. The key is to attach a statement to your tax return which discloses the nature and the amount of the excluded income. If the statement is adequate, the IRS will not consider the income to be omitted. Definitely consult an experienced tax preparer about the preparation of this statement.

No Return Filed—No Limit at All

If you simply fail to file your return for any year (and for any reason), the general three-year period never starts. In other words, there is no time limit that can expire before the IRS is stopped from challenging your return for that year. It doesn't matter whether your failure to file was deliberate or was due to an innocent oversight on your part.

Fraud! No Time Limit

If you file a return containing deliberate understatement of income or overstatement of deductions in order to reduce your tax liability, you may be charged with fraud. If the IRS can successfully establish fraudulent intent on your part, there is no time limit that stops the IRS from auditing your tax return and assessing additional tax.

You Might Agree to Extending the Time Limit

Very often the IRS will ask you to agree to extend the statutory period for a given year by entering into a written agreement to do so. This agreement is valid only if it is signed before the end of the regular statutory period for such year. As a practical matter, it will generally happen when the regular statutory period (either three or six years) is about to expire and the IRS considers additional time is necessary in order to be able to audit the return adequately.

Ordinarily, it is IRS policy to request an extension only when necessary and only for a reasonable period of time to complete the work. Keep in mind that you do not have to consent to such an agreement. It is strictly voluntary on your part. However, if you refuse to agree to the extension, the IRS, in order to protect their position, may simply assess a tax deficiency in some arbitrary amount before the end of the regular statutory period. You will then have to take your case to Administrative Appeals. Naturally, this arbitrary amount is likely to be at least as large, and probably much larger, than the maximum amount they might anticipate assessing after a complete audit. It is therefore generally recommended that the IRS be given an extension, but only for a limited time period. Again, be sure to consult an experienced tax representative before you make any decision on this one.

Once Tax Assessed—On to Collection

Once a tax has been properly assessed, the IRS generally has a ten year period after the date of assessment to collect the tax. In those relatively rare circumstances when the IRS has been unable to collect within this lengthy period of time, the IRS and the taxpayer could agree to an extension of time beyond the end of the ten-year period. You might wish to agree to such an extension to avoid the imposition of a lien on your property or wages. Alternatively, think seriously about an Offer in Compromise.

Caution: Things Can Get Much More Complex

The above discussion explains the general rules regarding the allowable time periods for the IRS to assess and collect a tax deficiency. In practice, these rules cover the vast majority of actual situations. However, there are a variety of special circumstances in which either:

1. The running of the period of limitation is suspended temporarily; or

2. An erroneous treatment of an item may be corrected even though it occurred in a year otherwise closed by the general rules.

Since these special circumstances occur only rarely at best, this book will not burden you with the unduly complex rules which apply in such situations.

CHAPTER 8

PROBLEM RESOLUTION PROGRAM

Solving Administrative Glitches And Hardship Cases

Problem Resolution Program

(Special Help for Special Problems)

In an effort to provide relief to taxpayers for some of the frustrations inevitably generated by a large and bureaucratic tax system, the IRS has created some safety valves. The Problem Resolutions Program (PRP) was implemented to give taxpayers a way to solve certain problems that seem to be going nowhere through the normal channels. Generally, these "problems" would be administrative or cause (or potentially cause) you a significant hardship.

Examples of Problems That Can Be Solved

Administrative

- The IRS owes you a refund that is overdue. The PRP officer will track your refund in the system.

- You continue to receive billing for a tax bill that has been paid. The PRP officer can determine why your payment was not properly credited to your account.

Significant Hardship

- You owe the IRS money and your payment schedule could cause a substantial hardship such as the deprivation of minimum necessities—food, shelter, clothing, medical treatment, utility shutoff, ability to keep a job, etc.

Examples of Problems That Cannot Be Solved

- You are not happy with the outcome of your audit. Administrative appeals and tax court are the correct forums for this problem.

Problem Resolution Program

- The IRS has levied your bank account but the levy (and as unhappy as you may be about it) will not cause "significant hardship."

Jack
(A Sad Story)

Jack was furious that his tax return was selected for audit by the IRS. He felt it was an inconvenience and unfair that he was being audited while his next door neighbor had never been audited. When the examining IRS agent disallowed certain deductions on his tax return, Jack immediately called Problem Resolutions. The IRS agent at Problem Resolutions politely informed Jack that he would have to take his case to administrative appeals.

Jack
(A Glad Story)

Jack paid the balance of the tax due on his tax return when he filed his return on April 15th. Somehow Jack did not receive credit for his final payment and he kept receiving computer-generated letters from the IRS demanding payment. Each letter was more threatening than the previous letter. Jack had called the local IRS office on several occasions but just could not get the problem resolved. Jack called Problem Resolutions and an agent Jack talked to was able to track Jack's payment through the system and solve the problem.

If you believe that you have a problem that is either an administrative glitch or a hardship case you can either:

> Call toll free 1 (800) 829-1040 and speak directly to a Problem Resolution officer

> or

Complete Form 911, application for taxpayer assistance to relieve hardship. Form 911 is available at your local IRS office.

If you qualify for assistance (and this is by no means automatic) the taxpayer Ombudsman (an Ombudsman is defined as someone who investigates complaints and helps to achieve equitable settlements) may issue a Taxpayer Assistance Order (TAO) to temporarily stop, or modify, further IRS action.

CHAPTER 9

OFFER IN COMPROMISE

The IRS Program For Settling Debts

You May Be Able To Settle For A Fraction
Of What You Owe

Offer In Compromise

(Let's Make a Deal)

Very often a taxpayer owes such a large amount of money to the IRS that, realistically, the bill will never get paid. In such dire times, Internal Revenue Code Section 7122 provides for the acceptance of a lesser amount as full payment of the tax due providing either one (or both) of the following situations exist.

1. **There is doubt as to whether the liability is really owed.**

2. **You do not have enough money to pay the tax bill and there is no reasonable prospect that you will have the money in the foreseeable future.**

As a practical matter, the inability to pay the tax is almost always the reason for submitting an offer in compromise.

How Good of a Deal Can be Made?

A very good deal indeed! You may be able to settle for less than fifteen cents on the dollar (including penalties and interest). A $100,000 liability could be settled in full for as little as $15,000. While it is possible to settle for less than 15%, the IRS will reject offers it considers to be frivolous or less than could be collected by other means. However, the amount of money you offer the IRS must be equal to your net worth, except for nominal personal effects such as clothing, furniture, etc. If the offer is accepted, the slate will be clean. You won't own anything but you won't owe anything to the IRS.

Jack and Jill do a Deal

Jack and Jill have cash in their bank account of $8,000, a cash surrender value on Jack's life insurance policy of $2,000, and they own a house with a value of $100,000. There is a mortgage on the house of $95,000. They owe the IRS $100,000 for back taxes, penalties and interest. Jack has an ordinary job that manages to pay the bills. Jill does not work. Neither Jack nor Jill has any prospect of increasing their wealth in the foreseeable future. The offer compromise would be structured as follows:

Assets
- Cash in Bank .... $ 8,000
- Cash Surrender Value of Life
  Insurance   2,000
- Value of Home   100,000
Total Assets .... $ 110,000

Less: Mortgage Owed .... (95,000)
Net Worth .... $ 15,000

In this case Jack and Jill would offer $15,000 as full payment for back taxes of $100,000.

What If You Have Negative Net Worth?

If you have negative net worth and can borrow some money, you may be in an even stronger position with the IRS. The IRS may perceive that it has no chance of getting any money and something is better than nothing.

Jack and Jill Do a Better Deal

Jack and Jill only have $1,000 in cash, and a home worth $90,000. There is a mortgage on the home of $100,000. They owe the IRS $100,000 in back taxes, penalties and interest. Jack has an ordinary job that just manages to pay the bills and Jill does not work. There is no prospect that they will increase their wealth in the foreseeable future. In this case, Jack and Jill have negative net worth calculated as follows:

```
Cash  . . . . . . . . . . . . . . . . . .  $   1,000
Value of Home  . . . . . . . . . . . .     90,000
Total Assets  . . . . . . . . . . . . .  $  91,000

Less Mortgage on Home  . . . . . .   (100,000)
Negative Net Worth  . . . . . . . .  $ ( 9,000)
```

Jack and Jill are able to borrow $10,000 from friends and relatives. Jack and Jill would offer $10,000 to the IRS. There is an excellent chance the IRS will accept the offer.

In 1992, the IRS simplified the "Offer in Compromise" procedure. Since then, the number of "Offers in Compromise" has increased dramatically, both in terms of quantity and IRS acceptance. Beware, however! It may take up to a year for the IRS to make a decision; and interest and penalties continue to mount up.

How it is Done

You must fill out IRS Forms 656 and 433A. Form 656 is the Offer in Compromise Form where you list the tax liability, the amount of your offer and the reason for your offer. Form 433A is a comprehensive summary of your employment, personal and financial information. Additionally, the IRS will require supporting information such as recent tax returns, bank statements, mortgage papers, deeds to real estate, loan papers, etc.

Should a Tax Professional Help Fill Out the Forms?

Absolutely—Don't make a mistake at this point.

Does the IRS have to Accept the Offer?

No! The IRS will evaluate your offer. If, and only if, they think it is in their best interests will the offer be accepted. Naturally, the more money offered the more likely it will be accepted.

How is the Payment Made?

The IRS prefers to be paid in full at the time the Offer in Compromise is accepted. However, it is possible to work out an installment plan. Naturally, your offer is more likely to be accepted if you can pay the compromised amount in full at the time of acceptance.

Advantages and Disadvantages

Major Advantages

1. You can settle a large IRS bill for a small amount of money.

2. After you have agreed to a compromise amount **and** paid the amount, the IRS will remove any tax liens it has on your property and your credit rating will improve.

3. You will sleep better at night.

Major Disadvantages

1. You must file all returns when due and pay **all** taxes due for five years after the offer in compromise is accepted.

2. You waive all rights to contest in court, at a later date, the tax liability being compromised.

3. Once the compromise is accepted, you must not default on the terms of the agreement.

A failure to file returns and pay taxes on a timely basis, or a default in the agreement, may cause the IRS to terminate the agreement and assess the entire tax liability that was originally owed less any payments made.

CHAPTER 10

TRUST FUND RECOVERY PENALTY

Be Careful About Paying Payroll And Excise Taxes

Trust Fund Recovery Penalty

While the IRS is serious about receiving payment on all taxes due, there is a particular sensitivity to trust funds. Trust funds are funds collected by one party (an employer) from another party (usually an employee) to be paid to the IRS. They are called trust funds because the party collecting the funds never owned the money but rather temporarily held the money "in trust" until it was sent to the IRS. Trust funds are employment taxes (including Income Tax Withheld), the employee—but not employer—portion of FICA taxes, Railroad Retirement taxes and collected Excise Taxes.

Since all trust funds are kept by the business until paid to the IRS, it is tempting for businesses short on cash to use the money to pay other creditors. It may be several months before the IRS realizes that they have not received payment.

Illustration:

Jack and Jill own a small business with one employee. Every week their employee receives a net paycheck. The amount of the net paycheck is calculated by determining gross pay and then deducting federal income tax and FICA tax. The federal income tax and the employee's portion of the FICA tax are trust funds. Jack and Jill are required to remit this money to the IRS. If Jack and Jill fail to send the trust funds to the IRS, they will be subject to the trust fund recovery penalty. The amount of the penalty is 100% of the unpaid trust fund tax. In other words, the IRS will seek to recover all of the unpaid trust funds. To be liable for the penalty the factors of **responsibility** and **willfulness** must be present.

Who is Responsible?

Broadly speaking a responsible person is one who has an obligation to see that the tax is remitted and has the authority to remit the tax. This responsibility is not limited to the owner of a business but may include directors, officers, employees, trustees, or any other person with authority or control over the cash account.

What is Willfulness?

Willfulness is the intentional disregard of the law. The IRS defines willfulness as:

"Conduct that is intentional, deliberate, voluntary and knowing."

Typically, willfulness exists where a responsible person knows that unpaid taxes exist and allows (even tacitly) the funds to be used to pay other creditors. Willfulness cannot exist if a potentially responsible person did not have knowledge of an unpaid tax liability. However, at the instant in time that a responsible person becomes aware of unpaid tax, he can be held responsible for every payment from that point forward to creditors other than the IRS.

Unwillful Jack Unwittingly Becomes Willful Jack

Jack received a call from his friend and fellow board of director member, Don. Don asked Jack to attend a meeting with the IRS. At the meeting with the IRS, Don explained to Jack that the company was behind in payroll taxes totaling $100,000, but that the IRS agent had agreed to an installment plan so that the business would not have to be closed. Up to this point Jack had not been aware that payroll taxes had not been paid. The plan called for monthly installment payments of $10,000. Two months later the plan failed and the IRS closed the business. The IRS assessed Jack for $80,000.

Jack's CPA explained to Jack that during the two-month period, the company had receipts of $100,000 and, as agreed, paid $20,000 to the IRS and the balance of $80,000 to other creditors. However, in spite of the agreement with the IRS to make installment payments, Jack was liable for every dollar paid to creditors after he became aware of the unpaid tax. The IRS agent did not explain this pitfall to Jack when they had their meeting.

Jack
(A Sad Story)

Jack recently retired and was flattered when his old army buddy, Don, asked him to become a member of the Board of Directors of his company. While the job only paid a few hundred dollars a year, Jack looked forward to the once-a-year meetings in a neighboring town. During the last meeting, Don (who was also president of the company) mentioned that the company was behind in the payment of its payroll taxes because the money was being used to pay other creditors. Jack listened but did not comment. Later, Jack was shocked when the IRS assessed him for the trust fund recovery penalty which was over $100,000. As things turned out, Don and the other Board members did not have any money, so the IRS assessed Jack for the entire amount. Jack's CPA explained that as a Director he could be held responsible and that by being silent when Don disclosed the non-payment of trust funds at the board meeting, he had given tacit approval to using the funds to pay other creditors.

Jack
(A Glad Story)

Jack recently retired and was flattered when his old army buddy, Don, asked him to become a member of the Board of Directors of his company. While the job only paid a few hundred dollars a year, Jack looked forward to the once-a-year meetings in a neighboring town. During the last meeting, Don (who was also president of the company) mentioned that the company was behind in the payment of its payroll taxes because the money was being used to pay other creditors. Jack was surprised and stated that he was not aware that there were unpaid payroll taxes. Jack immediately demanded that no other payments be made to other creditors until the payroll taxes were paid. Jack also resigned as a Director in protest of the non-payment of the trust fund taxes. Later, Don and the other board members were assessed 100% penalty, but Jack was not. The IRS could not establish that Jack had willfully allowed the payroll taxes to go unpaid.

Designate Payments to Protect Yourself

If the company should get behind in paying payroll taxes and subsequently begins to make catch-up payments, be sure to designate that the payments are to be used first to pay trust fund liabilities. If this is not specified in writing, the IRS has the right to apply the payments in any fashion it wants. Inevitably payment will be allocated to penalties, interest and other non-trust fund liabilities. This tactic allows the IRS continued ability to assert the trust fund penalty.

The Moral of the Story

Be extremely careful about accepting honorary positions such as Director of a company. Also, be wary of accepting the responsibility for signing checks in a business. If you can sign checks, you can pay payroll taxes. Failure to do so may be a willful act.

CHAPTER 11

BANKRUPTCY

Definition Of Bankruptcy

Administrative Procedures

Priority Claims

Types Of Bankruptcy

Income Taxes Discharged

Bankruptcy

No one sets out initially to place himself or herself in the position of being put into bankruptcy, either voluntarily or involuntarily (involuntarily means your creditors place you in bankruptcy). However, at some point in time you may find yourself so financially insolvent and burdened with debt that entering bankruptcy may be the only way to get a fresh start.

It is not within the scope of this chapter to cover in detail the rules and procedures involved in bankruptcy proceedings, nor to provide guidelines for determining the advisability of declaring bankruptcy or the type of bankruptcy to choose in any particular case. Rather the purpose here is to provide you with a general idea of what bankruptcy is all about, the various types of bankruptcy available to individuals, and how your federal income tax obligations will be treated during and after the close of bankruptcy proceedings. If you decide to seek the protection of bankruptcy laws, you should consult an attorney.

What is bankruptcy all about?

The purpose of bankruptcy laws is to provide a way for persons heavily overburdened with debt to get a "fresh start." When you file your petition with the bankruptcy court, you place your assets and/or your business under the control and protection of the court. During the bankruptcy period, your creditors cannot harass you for payment; they must make their claims for payment through the court. Automatically, the filing of a petition of bankruptcy gives you breathing room.

If you file for a "liquidation bankruptcy," the court will allow you to keep a limited amount of certain types of property, which is referred to as **exempt property**. The **nonexempt property** will be sold by a court-appointed trustee to pay off your creditors.

If you file under any of the other three types of reorganization bankruptcy (discussed in more detail later), you may be able to retain your property as long as you come up with an acceptable plan to pay off all or part of your debts over a reasonable and specified period of time.

Regardless of which type of bankruptcy you file for, you will generally receive a discharge from your unsecured debts which remain unpaid at the close of bankruptcy. **Discharge** means that the debt is eliminated; you are no longer under a legal obligation to pay it. However, there are a number of types of debt which are not dischargeable in bankruptcy and you are still legally obligated to pay them after your bankruptcy case is closed. This chapter focuses specifically on how your Federal income tax debts are treated: i.e., whether they are subject to discharge or not. Treatment of other types of debt is not covered.

Before considering the nature of the four types of bankruptcy and their effect as to discharge of Federal income tax debt, however, we should understand the following basic concepts which are involved to a greater or lesser degree in all four types:

- **The Automatic Stay**
- **The Bankruptcy Estate**
- **Bankruptcy Schedules**
- **Prioritizing Creditor Claims**

The Automatic Stay

Upon filing the bankruptcy petition with the bankruptcy court, you are immediately granted an **automatic stay**. This means in general that your creditors, including the IRS, may not take direct action against you to collect outstanding debts. Instead they must file their claims with the court and seek payment in accordance with the priority assigned to their claims under the plan confirmed by the court.

The Bankruptcy Estate

Know the Difference between Exempt and Nonexempt Assets

When you file for bankruptcy, your property comes under the control of the bankruptcy court and is generally referred to as the **bankruptcy estate**. Your property is subject to: sale to provide money to pay creditors; transfer to lienholders to satisfy their liens; or, in the case of business assets, possibly retention for continued use in your business. The key point is that the actual use of the property will be under the control and approval of the court. You no longer control your assets and you cannot dispose of them without court approval.

However, if you were to be stripped of **all** of your assets, you would undoubtedly find it difficult to get the "fresh start," which is a major objective of the bankruptcy laws. Accordingly, Federal bankruptcy law specifies certain property as being **exempt** from bankruptcy—that is, you can keep it. In addition, the states also have property exemption laws which list properties which cannot be taken from you by creditors. The types and the amounts of these exempt properties differ widely, as between Federal and state and as amongst the various states. If your state has not opted out of the Federal exemptions, you will have a choice of utilizing either the Federal or state exemptions, whichever is more favorable to you. If your state has opted out, you have to go with the state exemptions.

Typical exemptions, subject to certain dollar limitations, are your residence, a motor vehicle, household furnishings, clothing, books, some jewelry, work tools, etc. If you should decide on filing for bankruptcy, you should find out beforehand what types and amounts of assets you can claim as exempt, so that you can plan accordingly.

Bankruptcy Schedules

Soon after filing the petition (usually within 15 days), you must complete and file with the court various schedules which list all your properties, your liabilities (including names and addresses of your creditors), and your current income and expenses. The court will then notify the creditors of the bankruptcy action so they can file appropriate proofs of their claims against you. You should make every effort to be complete in identifying any actual or contingent claims. If you fail to list a particular claim so that the creditor is not notified of your bankruptcy, this may cause the claim to survive after the bankruptcy when it might otherwise have been discharged.

Prioritizing Creditor Claims

Those claims of creditors with the highest priority are to be paid first from the available assets or income. The remaining assets or income will be used to pay claims at the next level of priority, and so on, until all available assets and/or income have been exhausted.

From highest to lowest, the order for priority of payment may be summarized as follows:

Secured Creditor Claims

Unsecured Creditor Claims
  Priority Claims—First through Ninth Priority
  Non-Priority Claims—Other Unsecured Claims

Each of these categories is explained below.

Secured Creditor Claims

This category includes those claims which are secured by an interest in specific property or properties, such as a mortgage on your house. Thus it would include tax liens for Federal income tax liabilities which have been assessed, if the IRS has filed public notice of the lien.

Although not referred to technically as "priority claims," secured claims have the first right to be paid from the proceeds of a sale of the property securing the claim, or alternatively, in some cases, by transfer of ownership of the property to the secured creditor. Of course, if the sales proceeds or property value are less than the amount of the claim, the balance of the claim falls into the category of unsecured claims.

Unsecured Claims

Unsecured claims, on the other hand, are divided between those which have a specified priority with respect to the right to be paid (**priority claims**) and those which are **nonpriority claims**. This distinction is of particular importance because the nonpriority claims are more readily discharged in bankruptcy. Priority debt is more difficult to discharge or, in some cases, is not dischargeable at all.

Priority Claim Levels

The general category of unsecured debt qualifying as priority claims is further subdivided into nine so-called priority levels. This means that debts in the first priority are to be paid before those in second priority, and so on. The Federal income tax liabilities may fall within any one or more of the first, second, and eighth priority levels. Thus our discussion here is limited to those categories.

First Priority

Administrative expense claims. These are claims for expenses which arise in the administration of the bankruptcy procedure—such as any fiduciary, legal, or accounting fees for administrative services. Taxes incurred by the bankruptcy estate during the period of its administration would fall under the first priority—such as income taxes, employee federal income taxes withheld, etc.

Second Priority

This category generally applies only in the case of an **involuntary** bankruptcy filed against a business. It includes those expenses and unsecured claims which arise during the period between the date the involuntary bankruptcy is filed and the date when the bankruptcy court grants an order of relief whereby the operation of the business is placed under court supervision. Taxes incurred by the debtor during this period fall into this category.

Eighth Priority

This is the category which includes most unsecured tax claims. The income taxes which fall within this priority include the following:

a. **Three-year rule:** Income taxes for years that ended on or before the date the bankruptcy petition is filed, but only if the last due date (including extensions) for the return for such year fell within the three-year period preceding the date the petition is filed.

   Example: Assume you filed your 1993 Federal income tax return by its original due date, April 15, 1994. On January 12, 1995, the IRS assessed an additional $5,000 tax for 1993, which you have not paid. If your bankruptcy petition is filed on or before April 15, 1997 (i.e., within three years of your original, not extended, due date), this $5,000 tax liability falls within this category. If your petition was filed after April 15, 1997, the liability would not fall within this category.

If you had extended your original due date to August 15, 1994 and filed by that date, your tax liability would fall in this category only if your bankruptcy petition is filed on or before August 15, 1997 (i.e., within three years after the extended due date).

b. **240-day rule**: Income taxes for years not included in item (a) above if taxes were assessed within a 240 day period (or longer, where an offer in compromise is involved) preceding the date of filing the petition.

Example: Assume, as in the above example, that you filed your 1993 return by April 15, 1994; however, the IRS assessed the $5,000 additional tax for that year on February 10, 1997. If you file your bankruptcy petition on or before October 8, 1997 (240 days after the date of assessment), your $5,000 tax liability is eighth priority.

c. **Still assessable rule:** Income taxes for other years that were not assessed before, but were assessable as of, the date of filing the petition.

Example: Assume you filed your 1993 return by April 15, 1994. Ordinarily the IRS would have three years (until April 15, 1997) to assess any additional tax for that year. However, at the request of the IRS, you signed an agreement on February 15, 1997 to extend the period for assessment until April 15, 1998. Assume the IRS assessed the additional $5,000 tax on November 3, 1997. If you file your bankruptcy petition on May 30, 1997, the November 3, 1997 assessment does not fall within either the three year test in item (a) above or the 240 day test in item (b) above. However, though not assessed on the petition's filing date, it was still assessable because of the extension agreement, and therefore, it still falls within the eighth priority.

Exceptions: Certain situations which would meet the "still assessable" test are specifically excluded from the eighth priority. These situations cover income taxes for years for which **no return** was filed, a **fraudulent return** was filed, or a **late return** (filed within two years of filing the bankruptcy petition) was filed. As explained later, Federal income tax liabilities falling within these exceptions are generally not dischargeable except in the case of so-called Chapter 13 bankruptcies.

Non-Priority Unsecured Claims

Those unsecured claims, including income taxes, not included in any of the nine priority levels are last in line for payment—that is, if there's anything left.

Types of Bankruptcy

The controlling rules for bankruptcy (the Bankruptcy Code) are found primarily in Title 11 of the United States Code, which is divided into a number of chapters. An individual potentially may file under any one of four types of bankruptcy, each type being covered in a separate chapter (Chapters 7, 11, 12, and 13) of the Bankruptcy Code.

Chapter 7—Liquidation Bankruptcy
(Your Assets are Sold and Creditors are Paid)

A trustee is appointed to take control of all the nonexempt assets (the bankruptcy estate) of the bankrupt debtor and to supervise the bankruptcy procedure. In the case of property with a lien on it, such as a mortgage on your house, the trustee may choose to transfer the house back to the lienholder. The rest of the nonexempt assets are sold by the trustee who then disburses the proceeds to pay those claims allowed by the court in the order of their priority. In most circumstances, the court will then discharge (eliminate) any remaining unpaid debts to the extent they are dischargeable. The automatic stay is then terminated and the trustee files his final report of the distribution with the court.

Discharge of Unpaid Tax

As a general rule, most unpaid unsecured regular debt is discharged in bankruptcy; however, there is generally **no discharge** at the termination of a Chapter 7 bankruptcy case for the following income tax liabilities:

1. **Second priority taxes:** Taxes incurred by the debtor between the date an **involuntary** bankruptcy is filed against the debtor's business and the date the operation of the business is placed under court supervision.

2. **Eighth priority taxes:** Tax liabilities for prior years whose last due date (**including extensions**) fell within the three-year period preceding the filing of the bankruptcy petition (**three-year rule**), and tax liabilities for earlier years if such taxes were actually assessed within the 240 day period preceding the filing of the petition (**240-day rule**), or, if not assessed, could have been assessed, on the filing date (**still assessable rule**).

3. Tax liabilities for which **no tax return** was filed.

4. Tax liabilities for which a **late return** was filed, if it was filed within two years of the date the bankruptcy petition was filed.

5. Tax liabilities with respect to which a **fraudulent return** was filed.

Claims against you for other income taxes predating the bankruptcy petition by more than three years may be discharged. In summary, the only Federal income tax liabilities discharged in a **liquidation** bankruptcy are those which fall **outside** the scope of all of the following:

- **Three-year rule**
- **240-day rule**
- **Still assessable rule**
- **Late return—2 year rule**
- **Fraudulent return**
- **No return**

In brief, most Federal income tax liabilities are **not** discharged in a **liquidation-type** bankruptcy.

This conclusion may be best illustrated by describing Jack and Jill's tax plight in their Chapter 7—Bankruptcy Liquidation.

Jack and Jill in a Liquidation Bankruptcy
(Most Income Tax Liabilities Survive)

Jack and Jill filed their petition for bankruptcy under Chapter 7 (the liquidation-type bankruptcy) on June 10, 1995. They have had an unusual variety of circumstances over the years with respect to their Federal income taxes (see next page).

100   The IRS And You

Taxable Year	Status
1994	Return timely filed on April 10, 1995. All tax paid. No tax deficiency.
1993	Return timely filed (under extension to August 15, 1994) on June 12, 1994. On March 3, 1995, IRS assessed a tax deficiency of $1,200, which has not been paid.
1992	Return timely filed on April 3, 1993. All tax paid. No tax deficiency.
1991	Received filing extension to August 15, 1992. Return timely filed on August 11, 1992. On July 7, 1994, IRS assessed a tax deficiency of $1,500, which hasn't been paid.
1990	Return timely filed on March 30, 1991. IRS assessed a tax deficiency of $2,000 on July 7, 1994, which hasn't been paid.
1989	Return timely filed on April 14, 1990. The 3-year statute of limitations for a tax assessment would have expired on April 15, 1993. However, on April 10, 1993 Jack and Jill signed an agreement with the IRS to extend the statute to August 30, 1995. IRS assessed a tax deficiency of $1,100 on August 14, 1995.
1988	No return ever filed.

Tax Discharge Status:

Taxable years 1994, 1993 and 1992: Tax liability not discharged—Three-year rule applies. The last due date for returns for these years (April 15, 1995, August 15, 1994—the extended due date, and April 15, 1993 respectively) all fall within the three-year period preceding the bankruptcy filing date—June 10, 1995. Thus they all clearly fall within the category of **eighth priority taxes.** But priority taxes are not discharged in bankruptcy. Thus any part of the $1,200 tax deficiency for 1993 not paid in the bankruptcy would survive the bankruptcy; that is, it would remain a liability of Jack and Jill.

Taxable year 1991: Tax liability not discharged—Three-year rule applies. The original due date for 1991 was April 15, 1992. But Jack and Jill got an extension to August 15, 1992. Since this extended due date falls within the three-year period preceding the bankruptcy filing, it also falls within the category of **eighth priority taxes**; so Jack and Jill will remain liable for any part of the 1991 deficiency of $1,500 which remains unpaid in the bankruptcy.

Note, however, that **if** Jack and Jill had delayed filing the bankruptcy petition until August 20, 1995, then the extended due date of August 15, 1992 would not fall within the prior three years; thus the three-year rule would not have applied. Also, since IRS assessed the 1991 tax deficiency on July 7, 1994, this assessment date was more than 240 days before the bankruptcy filing date; thus it would not be a priority tax under the 240-day rule either. So the tax deficiency would not be a priority tax. Therefore, assuming the return was not a fraudulent one, any unpaid balance of the 1991 deficiency of $1,500 would have been discharged. This is just one indication of the need for early planning, even before a bankruptcy petition is filed.

Taxable year 1990: Tax liability discharged. The tax deficiency of $2,000 for 1990 is not a priority tax. It clearly does not fall under the three-year rule. Neither does it fall under the 240-day rule—**The assessment date of July 7, 1994 precedes the bankruptcy filing date of June 10, 1995 by more**

than 240 days. Therefore, assuming no fraudulent return, any unpaid balance of this deficiency is discharged.

By way of illustration, assume that Jack and Jill's return for 1990 was not filed until September 13, 1993—a late return filed within two years of the bankruptcy filing date of June 10. 1995. Although the $2,000 tax deficiency assessment would not be a priority tax, it would not be discharged because it would fall under the **late return-two year rule.**

Taxable year 1989: Tax liability not discharged—Tax was not assessed, but was **still assessable** as of June 10, 1995 when the bankruptcy petition was filed. The tax deficiency of $1,100 for 1989 obviously doesn't fall under the three-year rule. Neither does it fall under the 240-day rule, since the tax was assessed on August 14, 1995, which date is **after** June 10, 1995 when the bankruptcy petition was filed. However, it is a priority tax under the **still assessable** test. Through several extensions, Jack and Jill had given the IRS until August 30, 1995 to assess a tax deficiency for 1989. Thus the tax, though not assessed, was **still assessable** at June 10, 1995, the bankruptcy filing date.

Taxable year 1988: Tax liability not discharged—No return filed. If the IRS assesses a tax deficiency for 1988, it will not be a priority tax. Nevertheless, the liability will not be discharged in bankruptcy because of the **no return filed** test.

As this illustration shows, you may not get much relief from Federal income tax liabilities in a Chapter 7 bankruptcy, except in unusual circumstances. If you can qualify for a Chapter 13 bankruptcy, you can get a better break.

Chapter 13—Wage-Earners Bankruptcy

This form of bankruptcy is available only to individuals. It allows you to keep your property, rather than having it taken over by the trustee for liquidation. Specifically, this is a reorganization whereby you pay your debts over an extended period of time. To qualify, however, you must be able to demonstrate that you have a regular and stable income, and can propose a realistic plan for the full or partial repayment of debts over a period of three (or, in some cases, up to five) years. Further, your secured debt must be less than $750,000 and your unsecured debt must be less than $250,000. If you are in business as a sole proprietor and you meet the above qualifications, you can use Chapter 13 as a business bankruptcy.

Assuming you qualify, you will be required to prepare a budget of sorts, which lists your income and essential living expenses and a schedule for debt repayments with the remaining money. Ordinarily, the plan must provide for **full payment of priority claims, including priority taxes**, unless your creditor (including the IRS) agrees to a lesser amount. In addition, the value of the property to be distributed under the plan to each unsecured creditor must not be less than the amount which the creditor would receive if your estate were liquidated in a Chapter 7 bankruptcy. If the court approves your plan, you will make the scheduled monthly payments to an appointed trustee, who then makes the payments to the creditors.

After all payments under the plan have been made successfully, the court will grant you a discharge from almost all remaining unpaid debts covered in the plan, including those prepetition taxes not dischargeable in a Chapter 7 bankruptcy (see listing above). In other words, generally you will be required to provide in your plan for full payment of your priority taxes, which includes those falling within the **three-year rule, the 240-day rule**, or the **still assessable rule**. But you will be discharged from other unpaid Federal income tax liabilities, even though they fall within the scope of the **fraudulent return, no return**, or **late return/2-year rule**.

If you fail to make all the bankruptcy plan payments, under certain limited circumstances the court may still grant you a discharge. However, the debts discharged are only those which would be discharged in a Chapter 7 liquidation bankruptcy. Thus tax liabilities for priority taxes, or for taxes for which no return, a late return (filed within two years of your bankruptcy filing date), or a fraudulent return was filed would not be discharged.

If you fail to make all the payments and do not meet the limited circumstances required for a discharge, your Chapter 13 bankruptcy will be dismissed or converted to a Chapter 7 liquidation bankruptcy.

Most individuals who file bankruptcy do so under either the Chapter 7 or Chapter 13 types explained above. However, where the particular circumstances fit, you may also file under Chapter 11 or Chapter 12.

Chapter 11—Reorganization Bankruptcy

This form of bankruptcy is really designed to be a reorganization plan (as opposed to a liquidation of assets) for businesses. As explained above, an individual operating a business as a sole proprietor can file under Chapter 13, but only if its restrictive qualification requirements are met. Otherwise, Chapter 11 may be the only way to keep the business from being liquidated.

However, you can also file under Chapter 11 for yourself, even if you are not in business. For example, you might not meet the qualifications for a Chapter 13 bankruptcy, and you don't want to give up your nonexempt assets which would be liquidated in a Chapter 7 bankruptcy. A Chapter 11 bankruptcy could be your only alternative for holding on to the nonexempt assets.

In either case, a Chapter 11 bankruptcy is usually more complex and expensive than one under Chapter 7 or 13. Due to its complexity and limited use by individuals, no attempt is made here to describe its procedures. You should note, however, that the rules for discharging taxes are the same for a Chapter 11 bankruptcy as for a Chapter 7 bankruptcy.

Chapter 12—Family-Farmer Bankruptcy

This form of bankruptcy was first made available by legislation enacted in 1986 in reaction to the increased number of foreclosures on small farming operations. It is fashioned pretty much in the manner of a Chapter 13 bankruptcy, allowing the debtor to retain possession and control of his/her property, while paying off the creditors under a deferred payment plan, over a period of three to five years. However, it has its own set of restrictive requirements as to which farmers can qualify to use it. In general terms, this type is available only for certain family-owned, smaller farm or ranch activities. The qualifications for Chapter 12 are as follows:

1. Total debts of the individual (or individual and spouse) engaged in the farming operation do not exceed $1,500,000.

2. At least 80% of the debts (excluding generally debts for the residence of the individual or the individual and his spouse), on the date the case is filed, arose out of the farming operations owned and operated by such individuals.

3. For the taxable year preceding the bankruptcy filing date, more than 50% of the gross income of the individual (or individual and spouse) was received from such farming operation.

As in the case of a Chapter 13 bankruptcy, the appointed trustee will collect the payments from you under the plan and then pay your creditors. When the payments under the plan are completed, the court will grant the debt discharge. However, unlike the Chapter 13 bankruptcy, the unpaid debts which survive a Chapter 7 and Chapter 11 bankruptcy also survive a Chapter 12 bankruptcy.

Dischargeability of Interest

Although the bankruptcy code does not specifically cover the subject, the courts generally agree that **pre-petition interest** (i.e., interest accrued before the bankruptcy petition is filed) on a tax liability carries the same priority as the tax claim itself. Thus pre-petition interest on a tax arising within three years of the bankruptcy filing date (**three year rule**) is not discharged in bankruptcy since it carries the same priority as the tax liability itself. On the other hand, an unassessed tax not due within three years of the bankruptcy filing date that is still assessable because of failure to file does not have priority status. Since such nonpriority tax is dischargeable under a Chapter 13 bankruptcy, but not under a Chapter 7 liquidation bankruptcy, any related pre-petition interest is also dischargeable under the Chapter 13, but not under the Chapter 7, bankruptcy.

Post-petition interest (interest accrued after the bankruptcy filing date), on the other hand, does not have priority status, whether it relates to priority or nonpriority tax claims. In a Chapter 7 liquidation bankruptcy, such interest due to nondischargeable taxes still survives the bankruptcy. Its treatment under a Chapter 13 bankruptcy, however, differs. Generally a Chapter 13 repayment plan requires that the present value of payments to be received over the life of the plan must at least equal the amount it would have received under a Chapter 7 straight liquidation. If the present value of the payments would be less than such straight liquidation amount, post-petition interest can be added to the payments required. To the extent any post-petition interest on an unsecured tax claim is not included in the plan requirements, it is discharged so long as the plan is successfully completed. Since the taxpayer filing bankruptcy usually has few assets, their liquidation value will most likely be less than the present value of payments from the taxpayer's future earnings; under such circumstances, no post-petition interest should be required even for priority tax claims.

Dischargeability of Penalties

Penalties do not have priority status, even when they relate to priority tax claims. If unsecured by a tax lien, they fall into the category of general unsecured nonpriority creditors. If the underlying tax claim is discharged, of course, the related penalty is also discharged. If the underlying tax claim is not dischargeable, treatment of the related penalty differs between Chapter 7 and Chapter 13 bankruptcies.

Under a Chapter 13 plan, the debtor's disposable income (future earnings during plan period less reasonable living expenses) must first satisfy all unsecured priority claims. Unsecured nonpriority creditors will be paid only to the extent of any remaining disposable income; any unpaid balances are dischargeable. Since tax penalties are nonpriority claims, they may be partly or fully discharged where taxpayer's disposable income is insufficient to satisfy all unsecured priority and nonpriority claims.

Under a Chapter 7 plan, a tax penalty related to a nondischarged tax is discharged only if the penalty applies to a transaction or an event that occurred prior to three years before the filing of the bankruptcy petition. For example, a tax penalty for fraud with respect to a return due within the three year period before the bankruptcy filing date is not discharged. If the return due date preceded the filing date by more than three years, a related tax fraud penalty (but not the tax itself) is discharged.

Summary

Title 11 (the Bankruptcy Code) of the United States Code is divided into a number of chapters. The four different types of bankruptcy are described in four separate chapters of Title 11:

Chapter 7—Liquidation

Chapter 13—Wage Earner Deferred Payment Plan

Chapter 12—Family-Farmer Deferred Payment Plan

Chapter 11—Business Reorganization

Depending upon his/her particular circumstances, an individual may qualify under any one of the four bankruptcy types. Because of the qualification requirements, most individuals will likely file under the rules for Chapter 7 liquidation plan or the Chapter 13 wage-earner deferred payment plan. However, the Chapter 11 reorganization plan or Chapter 12 family-farmer plan may be more suitable if you meet their more restrictive requirements.

Under all of these plans, if the bankruptcy is carried out successfully, most unsecured regular debt will be discharged, such as unsecured charge card debts, medical bills and bank loans. But under Chapter 7, 11 and 12 bankruptcies, among the debts which survive bankruptcy are income taxes:

1. For the three years preceding the bankruptcy filing date;

2. For earlier years where either:

   - No return was filed;

   - The return filed was either fraudulent or filed late (within 2 years of bankruptcy filing date);

   - The tax was assessed within 240 days before the bankruptcy filing date; or

   - The tax, though not assessed yet, was assessable on the bankruptcy filing date (e.g., because you signed an extension agreement.)

Under a Chapter 13 bankruptcy, you can be discharged from all of these unpaid taxes which remain, if your deferred-payment plan was confirmed by the court and all payments provided for in the plan are timely made. However, your deferred-payment plan must provide for full payment of the priority tax liabilities (unless the IRS agrees otherwise), or your plan will not be confirmed by the bankruptcy court. Thus generally it is only the unpaid non-priority tax liabilities which will be discharged.

Once again, a caution! The bankruptcy laws and procedures are complex and subject to change. Advance planning can be crucial. For the most favorable results, consult with a knowledgeable attorney as soon as the likelihood of bankruptcy is reasonably foreseen.

CHAPTER 12

FRAUD

Definition Of Fraud

What Is Fraudulent

What Is Not Fraudulent

Criminal Investigations

The Penalty

Fraud

(Hire an Attorney Immediately)

While the overwhelming majority of IRS audits are routine civil examinations, occasionally fraud comes into the picture. It is often difficult for the public to understand the difference between routine civil audit adjustments to a tax return and allegations of fraud. There is, however, a vast difference between **avoiding** taxes and **evading** taxes.

Avoiding Taxes is Not Fraudulent

The Internal Revenue Manual briefly but eloquently distinguishes between tax avoidance and tax evasion in the following manner:

> "Avoidance of tax is not a criminal offense. **All taxpayers have the right to reduce, avoid, or minimize their taxes by legitimate means.** The distinction between avoidance and evasion is fine, yet definite. One who avoids tax does not conceal or misrepresent, but shapes and preplans events to reduce or eliminate tax liability, then reports the transactions."

It is perfectly legal, respectable, and admirable to pay the minimum amount of tax required by law. Tax law is complicated and not always clear-cut as to meaning. It is also possible to structure financial transactions in such a way that the amount of a tax liability might be reduced or even eliminated. A simple example is for a taxpayer to hold on to a stock investment in a corporation for more than a year and thereby take advantage of lower long term capital gain tax rates. In this illustration, the taxpayer is working within the framework of the tax law to **avoid** higher tax rates.

Evading Taxes is Fraudulent

"Evasion," on the other hand, the Internal Revenue Manual tells us, "involves deceit, subterfuge, camouflage,

Fraud

concealment, some attempt to color or obscure events, or making things seem other than they are."

However, the determination of fraud is not easy. The IRS must prove:

1. That the tax liability was understated and

2. That the understatement was due to deliberate intent to evade tax.

The key word is **intent**. The mere fact that a tax liability was understated does not constitute fraud. Intent means that you, the taxpayer, deliberately misrepresent an item(s) on your tax return in order to reduce or eliminate a tax liability.

Intent does not include the following:

1. An honest difference of opinion in the interpretation of tax law (that is why we have tax court).

2. You relied on the advice of your tax preparer in taking a deduction on your tax return that turned out to be an improper deduction.

3. You made an honest mistake in taking a deduction. For example, you deducted your automobile costs in driving to and from work, believing this was a legitimate business expense.

4. You were careless or even negligent when you prepared your tax return.

Intent Does Include the Following:

The establishment of fraud is a factual issue but it is nevertheless, an issue that is evaluated on a case-by-case basis. While there are no easily definable guidelines, the following scenarios indicate intent to evade tax:

1. Back dating or altering documents to provide a favorable tax treatment.

2. Filing a false return—you describe yourself as a consultant when in fact you are a drug dealer.

3. Understating your income—you had income from a business deal deposited in a foreign bank that was not reported on your tax return.

4. You did not file a tax return when you had income and were required to file.

Criminal Investigation Division (CID)
(The Police Force of the IRS)

Agents who investigate fraud are called Special Agents. Special agents are the policemen of the IRS. They are highly trained, sophisticated and they carry badges and guns.

The CID usually begins an investigation as the result of information it receives from one or more of the following sources:

1. **Contacts from citizens**—usually an ex-spouse, ex-lover, or unhappy business associate.

2. **Other Law Enforcement Agencies**—The FBI arrests a suspected drug dealer and discovers $200,000 in cash in his apartment.

3. **Referrals from Other IRS Divisions**—What started out as a routine civil examination turned into suspected fraud.

4. **Sting Operations**—Occasionally special agents conduct their own "Sting Operations."

5. **Newspaper Stories**—Accounts of embezzlement, theft, or unusual gains may arouse suspicion.

CID investigations begin with Special Agents interviewing everybody (except you, the taxpayer) who they believe may have information. This includes both business associates and friends. These investigations are extremely comprehensive and commonly last more than a year. By the time this part of the investigation is completed, the agents will have interviewed the taxpayer's banker, insurance agent, real estate broker, stockbroker, business associates, girlfriends/boyfriends, etc. When necessary, records will be subpoenaed. Special agents are intimidating and it is against the law to lie to a federal agent; so you can be sure that friends, associates, and lovers will tell all.

If you get feedback from your friends or business associates that they have been contacted by special agents and asked questions about you, you should immediately hire a criminal tax attorney. Do not, we repeat, do not under any circumstances ever talk directly with Special Agents. Do not get yourself into deeper trouble by attempting to tell your friends and business associates what to say to the agent.

After investigating around you, the CID will either drop its investigation (if there is no merit to the case) or contact you directly. If you are contacted by Special Agents and are the target of an investigation, the agent will read you your rights: you have the right to be silent, the right to an attorney and anything you say can and will be used against you, etc.

Deciding to Pursue a Case

The IRS is very selective about the cases they decide to prosecute for fraud. Their decision to pursue a case depends on many factors including:

1. **The amount of taxes involved.** Ordinarily, if the tax liability was less than $2,500.00, the IRS probably would not bother.

2. **Multi-Year Violations.** In order to establish intent, the IRS usually likes to see a repeat pattern over more than one year. If the violation takes place in a single year, it is much easier for the taxpayer to say it was accidental rather than intentional.

3. **Education of the taxpayer.** Educated people are presumed to be more aware of tax obligations. It is very difficult for a CPA or tax attorney to plead ignorance in tax matters.

4. **Age and Health.** The IRS is not insensitive to its image. Ordinarily, elderly persons or people with serious medical problems will not be prosecuted.

5. **The IRS expectation of getting a conviction.** The IRS only pursues cases it feels reasonably certain will result in a conviction, which is why their conviction rate is about 90%.

The Penalty
(Not Good)

Internal Revenue Code Sections 7201 through 7207 specify the penalties if you "attempt to evade or defeat tax." Maximum possible punishment includes $100,000 in penalties ($500,000 for corporations), the costs of the government prosecution and five years in prison.

Jack
(A Sad Story)

Jack was a joker and he was clever. He was a successful salesman and knew he could talk himself out of anything. When he received a notice that he was being audited by the IRS, he decided to represent himself. After all, the audit was a routine office examination. During the interview the IRS agent noticed that there was a sizable amount of interest income from a bank that did not appear on the tax return. The IRS knew this because banks are required to advise the IRS of interest paid to individuals.

"Why," the IRS agent asked, "wasn't the interest reported?"

Jack smiled broadly and said, "I guess you got me—if I knew you guys got all that information from the bank I would have reported it."

Jack was shocked when the IRS agent immediately terminated the routine audit and referred the case to the Criminal Investigative Division. Later, Jack's criminal defense lawyer explained to Jack that he had established intent to defraud by effectively saying he had willfully omitted the interest income from his tax return.

Jack
(A Glad Story)

Jack was a joker and he was clever. He was a successful salesman and he knew he could talk himself out of most situations. Nevertheless, when he received a notice from the IRS that he was being audited he decided to hire a CPA to represent him. Jack knew he was not a tax expert and he did not want to talk himself into a bad situation with the IRS.

During the interview, the IRS agent noticed there was a sizable amount of interest income from a bank that did not appear on Jack's tax return. The IRS knew this because banks are required to advise the IRS of interest paid to individuals.

"Why," the IRS agent asked, "wasn't the interest reported on Jack's tax return?"

Jack's CPA was honestly perplexed. "I don't know," he said, "Jack is not here today; however, my guess is that he forgot to include the interest. After all, Jack is a salesman and not an accountant."

The IRS agent realized that another audit was scheduled to begin in a few minutes and proposed that the interest be added to taxable income as a routine civil audit adjustment. Jack's CPA agreed. Jack's audit was over.

CHAPTER 13

RESOURCES

Useful IRS Publications At Your Fingertips

Taxpayer Assistance

Resources

List of Books

The Internal Revenue Service produces dozens of free tax publications. These booklets can be useful in providing guidance in specific areas. Many of these publications are available at your local IRS office. All publications are readily available by calling the IRS toll-free at 1 (800) 829-3676. The following list includes some of the more popular titles dealing with your rights as a taxpayer:

Publication Number	Title
1	Your Rights as a Taxpayer
556	Examination of Returns, Appeal Rights, and Claims for Refund
594	Understanding the Collection Process
908	Bankruptcy and Other Debt Cancellation
911	Application to Relieve Hardship
1546	How to Use the Problem Resolution Program of the IRS

Taxpayer Assistance Numbers

The telephone numbers of the Internal Revenue Service are listed in the white pages of your local telephone directory under U.S. Government, Internal Revenue Service. If you cannot find the number or address, try the following:

- Hearing Impaired with TDD access 1 (800) 829-4059

- Request Relief—Problem Resolutions 1 (800) 829-1040

- Application to Relieve Hardship 1 (800) 829-3676

Taxpayer Abroad

1. Contact the nearest U.S. Embassy.

2. Write:
   Internal Revenue Service
   Attention: IN:C:TPS
   950 L'Enfant Plaza South, S.W.
   Washington, D.C. 20024

About the Authors

Joseph F. Zerga, M.S., CPA

Mr. Zerga holds a Bachelors Degree (Summa Cum Laude) in Business Administration from Pace University in New York, and a Master's Degree in Accounting from the University of Nevada at Las Vegas. He is a former senior agent of the Nevada Gaming Control Board and currently is an adjunct faculty member at the University of Nevada.

Mr. Zerga is the Chief Executive Officer of Joseph F. Zerga, Ltd., a firm of Certified Public Accountants in Las Vegas, Nevada. He is also a licensed Certified Public Accountant in the state of Montana, and has authored numerous articles on taxation.

Richard J. Bannon, Ph.D., CPA

Mr. Bannon holds a Bachelors Degree (Summa Cum Laude) and a Doctors Degree in Economics from Catholic University of America in Washington, D.C. He is a former Professor of Accountancy and Taxation at DePaul University in Chicago, Illinois, where he initiated its Master's Program in Taxation. He also is a former tax partner with Arthur Young & Company (now Ernst and Young), an international firm of Certified Public Accountants.

Currently Mr. Bannon operates his own tax consulting service in Las Vegas, Nevada and has served as a lecturer in taxation at the University of Nevada at Las Vegas. He is a licensed Certified Public Accountant in Nevada and Illinois.

Index

adjustments. *See* tax adjustments
appeals
    administrative, 38-41, 45, 74
    court, 41-45, 74
assets, 48, 49, 50-52
    and bankruptcy, 90-91, 92, 93-94, 97-98, 102-103, 104, 105
    lack of, 49
attorneys, 26-27, 90, 109
audit
    avoiding, 17-18
    chances of, 12, 17, 18
    industry-specific guides, 24
    recording of, audio, 34-35
    repeat, relief from, 33-34
    selection process, 12-18
    stopping an in-progress, 35
automatic stay, 91

bank account levies, 51
bankruptcy, 52-53, 90-97, 106-109
    priority of claims, 93-97
    types of, 90-91, 97-108
burden of proof, 20, 35
business
    audit-intensive areas of, 16
    bankruptcy types and, 98, 103, 104
    field audit focus on, 23
    industry-specific guides, 24
    trust fund recovery penalty, 84-87

cash, businesses involving, 16
Certified Public Accountants (CPAs), 27
check signers, 87
CID. *See* Criminal Investigation Division
Claims Court, U.S., 40, 42-43, 43, 45
collection
    delayed, 49
    installment plans, 48-49, 52, 81
    ninety-day period and, 40
    sequence of action for, 49-52
    statute of limitations on, 71
complaints of taxpayer, 34

computer analysis, 12, 14-15
confidentiality, 33
correspondence audit, 21-22
costs
    of enforced collection, 50
    of tax representative, 31, 32
court appeals, 41-45
Court of Appeals, U.S., 43, 45
CPAs, 27
creditors. *See* bankruptcy
Criminal Investigation Division (CID), 114-116

deductions
    disallowed, 22, 39
    explanation of, 18, 65
    and intent to defraud, 113
    reporting of, 13, 14, 15
    unallowable, 12-14, 59
    See also supporting information
designated payment, 87
discharge of debt, 91, 98-102, 103-104, 105-109
Discriminant Function System (DFS), 14-15
District Court, 40, 42, 43, 45

emotions in process, 29, 31, 35, 41, 42
employment taxes, 84-87
enrolled agents, 27
errors, detection of, 12-14, 17
estimated tax penalty, 56-57
evasion of taxes, 112-114
examination. *See* audit
exempt assets, 90-91, 92
explanation, letter of, 14
extension for filing, 57-58, 60

fact pattern expression, 30
field audit, 23
filing date, official, 68
fraud, 112-118
    and bankruptcy, 97, 99, 103, 108
    and District Office requests, 17
    not focus of routine audit, 20
    penalties for, 66, 116-117

126 Index

and prison, 48
and statute of limitations, 70

hardship, 52, 75, 76, 121
honorary positions, 87

income
    estimated tax payments, 56-57
    interest on tax refund as, 59
    level, and audit chances, 18
    omission of, and limitation, 69
    reporting of, 13, 14
    See also wages
industry-specific audit guides, 24
information requests. *See* supporting information
information returns, discrepancies involving, 13
Information Returns Program, 13
installment plans, 48-49, 52, 81
intent, 113-114, 117
interest
    accrual of, 41, 42, 80
    dischargeability of, 106-107
    as mandatory, 57, 66
    paid on refunds, 56, 58-59
    on penalties, 61, 62, 63
    politics of, 59
    reporting on return, 13, 14, 21
    on tax, 56-58
Internal Revenue Code, 20, 79
Internal Revenue Service (IRS)
    audit selection process, 12-18
    criminal investigations by, 114-116, 117
    ignoring, caution against, 44
    objectives in seeking audit, 12, 15, 20
    rights of, 20, 34-35, 87
involuntary bankruptcy, 90, 95, 98
IRS agents
    Appeals Officers, 38-39
    relationship with, 22, 28, 29-30, 33
    Special Agents, 114-116
    and type of audit, 22, 23
IRS District Office, 14, 16-17
IRS Publications, 121

items, computer analysis of, 14-15

judges, 41, 42

levy, 50-52, 75
liens, 50

Market Segmentation Specialization Program, 24
Mathematical/Clerical Error Abatement Program, 12, 13-14

net worth, compromise based on, 78-80
ninety-day letter, 40-41
nonexempt assets, 90-91, 92
nonpriority claims, 94, 97
notification
    of audit, 20, 21, 22
    of bankruptcy, 93
    of deficiency, 40
    of IRS findings, 38
    of levy, 51, 52

offer in compromise, 52, 71, 78-82
office audit, 22
Ombudsman, 76

penalties, 59
    accrual of, 41, 42, 80
    accuracy-related, 65-66
    dischargeability of, 107
    failure to file on time, 60, 61-63
    failure to pay on time, 60-63
    fraud, 66
    frivolous returns, 66
    tax deficiency found, 64
    trust fund recovery, 84-87
    waiving
        bargaining, 66
        reasonable cause, 60, 62, 64
phone communication, 30, 32
pre-trial settlement, 41
priority of claims, 93-97
prison, debtors, 49
Problem Resolutions Program (PRP), 74-76

Index 127

property. *See* assets; real estate
proposals. *See under* tax adjustments
Pryor, David, 32

random selection for audit, 15-16
real estate seizure, 52
recording of audit, 34-35
refund claim
    and audit, 16
    and interest paid, 56, 58-59
    problem resolution and, 74
representation. *See* tax representative
responsiblity, 84-85
rights
    of IRS, 20, 34-35, 87
    of taxpayer, 32-35
    of tax representative, 26

scheduling, 22, 23, 35
selection process for audit, 12-18
settlement. *See* offer in compromise
Special Agents, 114-116
state income tax refund, 50
statute of limitations, 68-71
    extension of, voluntary, 70-71
Statutory Notice of Deficiency, 40-41
supporting information
    for offer in compromise, 80
    requested in audit, 22
    tax representative examining, 28
    with tax return, 15, 17-18, 65, 69
Supreme Court, U.S., 43-44, 45

tax adjustments
    first stage, 14
    proposed, 21-22
        disagreement with, 14, 21-22, 38
        requirements for, 35
    See also appeals
tax bill
    in correspondence audit, 21
    mathematical errors, due to, 13
    problem resolution, 74, 75
Tax Court, 40, 41, 42, 43, 45
taxes
    avoiding vs. evading, 112-114

    discharge of, 91, 98-102, 103-104, 105-109
    See also tax adjustments
Tax Measurement Compliance Program, 15-16, 17
taxpayer
    assistance numbers, 120-121
    address, change of, 40-41
    assembling data requested, 22, 31, 32
    ignoring the IRS, caution against, 44
    judicial inconsistency among, 43
    lifestyle changes required, 48
    options if unable to pay, 52-53
    presence of, at audit, 29-30
    rights of, 32-35
    self-representation, 29-30, 35
Taxpayer Assistance Order (TAO), 76
Taxpayer's Bill of Rights, 32-35
tax representative
    client assessment by, 30-31
    communication with, 30, 32
    consulting with, 69, 70-71, 80
    offices of, used for audit, 23
    rights and regulation of, 26
    right to, 34
    selection of and relationship with, 31-32
    as sole IRS contact, 23, 30
    types of, 26-27
    to avoid, 28-29
tax returns
    explanations attached to, 18, 65, 69
    linked to other individuals, 17
    none filed, 69-70, 97, 98, 99, 102, 103, 108, 114
    selection for audit, 12-18
thirty-day letter, 38
time
    advantages to taxpayer, 30
    appeals, 38, 40-41
    and bankruptcy, 93, 95-97, 98-102, 103, 106, 108
    extension for filing, 57-58
    IRS relation to, 22, 23
    liens and levies, 50, 51, 52

Index

    for offer in compromise, 80
    and penalties, 64
    statute of limitations, 68-71
trust fund recovery penalty, 84-87

Unallowable Items Program, 12, 13-14

wages
    levied, 50
    reporting, 13
    tax withholding, 56-57
willfulness, 84, 85-87

"Your Rights as a Taxpayer," 32

The IRS And You

To order additional copies of *The IRS And You: How To Play The Game And Win*, write, call, fax or e-mail Mainstream Press and request ordering information.

Mainstream Press
584 Castro Street, Suite 518
San Francisco, CA 94114 USA
Phone: 415-626-1867
Fax: 415-487-1137
E-Mail: 72114.2327@compuserve.com